Railway Age's

Comprehensive Railroad Dictionary

Technical and Contributing Editors

Robert G. Lewis, *Publisher, Railway Age*
Luther S. Miller, *Editor-In-Chief, Railway Age*
Gus Welty, *Senior Editor, Railway Age*
Kenneth G. Ellsworth, *Editor-In-Chief, The 1984 Car and Locomotive Cyclopedia*
Mason B. Flagg, *Assistant to Vice President-Equipment, Trailer Train Company*

Simmons-Boardman Books, Inc.
1809 Capitol Avenue, Omaha, Nebraska 68102

Railway Age's **Comprehensive Railroad Dictionary** is a guide to those words most commonly used in the railroad industry. No investigation has been made of common-law trademark rights in any word or term, because such an investigation would be impractical. The publisher is not responsible for any technical errors which might appear.

In the back of the book, a postcard is provided so that you can have personal input aimed at improving future editions of this "first" Comprehensive Railroad Dictionary. Thanks for your assistance.

First Printing: April, 1984
ISBN: 0-911382-00-3
Library of Congress Catalog Card Number: 83-051791

Publisher: Reid Kenedy
Managing Editor: Scott Sloan
Copy Editors: Dianna Adams, Jean Evers, Pat Giacalone, Joni Mulnix, Terri Polson

Foreword

Railway Age's **Comprehensive Railroad Dictionary** is the first dictionary compiled to include those words which are representative of all aspects of the modern railroad industry — mechanical, communications and signaling, track and structures, operations, and administration.

In publishing this dictionary, the intent has been to choose and define those words and terms that are indigenous to the railroad industry and have contemporary usage among professional railroad persons. As a result, this dictionary contains thousands of railroad vocabulary entries.

The wordstock of this industry includes a large body of slang, much of which has its roots in the steam era of railroading. Some slang terms are still in use (e.g., "highballing," "yellow eye," "green eye"), but the bulk have fallen out of usage. Compilations of railroad slang are available from a number of sources.

No attempt has been made to include the thousand or more electronics engineering terms which have applications in railroad communications equipment and installations using electronic data processing equipment, computers, and allied facilities and components.

A

"A" End of Car. A term used to identify locations on a car, being the end opposite the "B" end. The term is commonly seen with "L" or "R" to designate either left or right side, i.e. "AL" or "AR." See "B" End of Car.

"A" Unit. A diesel locomotive unit equipped with a cab and operating controls. Also called a "lead unit."

A.A.R. The Association of American Railroads. An industry association whose purposes include the promotion of railroad interests and the standardization and coordination of operating and mechanical activities within the railroad industry.

Abandonment (of Lines). As distinguished from curtailment, the complete cessation of service, operations, and maintenance of a railroad (usually a branch line), for which discontinuance permission has been granted by appropriate federal or state agency.

AB Brake. The standard freight car brake system which consists of the AB or ABD control valve, brake cylinder, auxiliary and emergency reservoirs, train line and other associated parts. The system allows rapid serial brake applications on each car in a train, controlled from the locomotive cab.

AB Brake Valve. The operating control valve of the AB freight-car brake, consisting of three portions: the service portion, the emergency portion, and the pipe bracket. The AB valve controls the charging, application and release of the air brakes on each car.

ABD Brake Valve. A modification of the AB Valve which is an integral part of the AB brake system for freight cars. The ABD valve substitutes certain internal parts, and features a quick release mechanism which facilitates rapid evacuation of air from the air brake cylinder.

ABDW Brake Valve. A further modification of the ABD valve involving a substitution of the emergency portion only. The ABDW valve provides accelerated buildup of brake cylinder pressure during service brake applications, and decreases the time required to achieve effective braking. The need for a B-1 quick service valve is eliminated when a car is equipped with the ABDW control valve.

Abrasion Plate. A special plate generally steel fabricated, used in special situations (in special track work and under continuous insulated joints) where a standard tie plate cannot be used. It is used to support the rail and prevent abrasion to the tie.

Absolute Block. A block in which no train is permitted to enter while it is occupied by another train, except as prescribed by the rules.

Absorption. Quantity of preservative solution absorbed by, or forced into a timber or tie during treatment. Volumetric absorption is the ratio of the absorption to the total volume of the timber.

Abstract of Freight Bills Issued. A self-balancing recapitulation of the freight bills issued by a station; used for accumulating information into daily and monthly totals for general records.

Abstract of Waybills. A brief or synoptical statement of waybills, distinguished as to waybills received or waybills forwarded; a report of freight received and dispatched from a station.

Abutment. A substructure composed of stone, concrete, brick or timber supporting the end of a span.

A.C. (a.c.). The abbreviation for alternating current.

Accessorial Service. A service rendered by a carrier in addition to a transportation service, such as assorting, packing, precooling, heating, storage, substitution of tonnage, etc.

AC/DC Motor. A series motor wound with compensating field coils, capable of operating with either alternating or direct current.

A.C. Floating Storage Battery System. A system wherein a combination of alternating current power supply, storage battery and rectifying devices are so made as to continuously charge the storage battery, and furnish power, at the same time for the operation of signal devices.

ACI (Automatic Car Identification). Any system to provide for automated identification of cars in a train. The most common uses a set of 13 reflective "modules" on each side of a car, caboose, locomotive, container, or trailer, which identifies the owner, number and equipment classification, when read by an optical scanner.

Acknowledger. A manually operated electric switch or pneumatic valve by means of which, on a locomotive equipped with automatic train stop or train control device, an automatic brake application can be forestalled, or by means of which, on a locomotive equipped with automatic cab signal device, the sounding of the cab indicator can be silenced. Sometimes called a "forestalling switch."

Acknowledging. The act of operating the acknowledger.

Acknowledging Time. As applied to an intermittent automatic train stop system, a predetermined time within which an automatic brake application may be forestalled by means of the acknowledging device.

Acknowledgment Circuit. A circuit consisting of wire or other conduction material installed between the track rails at each signal in territory where an automatic train stop system or cab signal system is in service, to enforce acknowledgment by the engineman at each signal displaying an aspect requiring a stop.

Acre. As measured along railroad right-of-way, 8 ft., 3 in. wide by 1 mile long.

Adapter (General). A device to serve the purpose of fitting one piece of apparatus to another.

Adapter, Base. A device used to mount a ground mast base for signal on a foundation designed for an instrument or mechanism case, or for mounting a single mechanism case on a double case foundation, or vice versa.

Adapter, Pipe. A device to permit mounting apparatus of a given size on pipe of a larger or smaller diameter.

Adapter, Roller Bearing. A casting that fits between a freight car roller bearing and the truck side frame to transfer the load from the side frame to the bearing.

Adhesion (of Drivers). A measure of the ability of locomotive driving wheels to accept rotational force without slipping on rails, usually expressed as a percent of the total weight on the drivers.

Adhesion Coefficient. The percent of the total weight on the driving wheels of a locomotive that is available for traction. It is largely dependent on the condition of the rail, and can vary from a low of 10% (.10) on wet rail to a high of 40% (.40) on dry sanded rail. Average coefficient of adhesion is about .25.

Adjusting Screw. A threaded device by means of which adjustments may be made to another mechanism.

Administrative Rulings. Informal rulings or opinions issued by the Interstate Commerce Commission.

Admixture (Construction). Any mixture added to the concrete mixture (other than cement, water, or aggregate) to accomplish certain changes in the properties of the concrete.

Advance (Internal Combustion Engines). Sometimes referred to as "lead or angle of advance," meaning the distance ahead of top or bottom dead center of the piston as measured in degrees of crank travel.

Advance Billing. A transfer of charges due to an error in billing a shipment. Example: Shipment was originally billed "collect" when it should have been billed "prepaid." Agent at originating point requests that charges be advanced back.

Advance Charges. Charges advanced by one carrier to another, and so on to the delivering carrier, for services performed in transporting the shipment.

Advance of a Signal. The side of the signal opposite from which the aspect is viewed. Example: the derailment occured 400 yards in advance of signal 132.6.

Adverse Dynamic Behavior. Any motion which is unfavorable to the movement of trains or individual cars, including rock-

and-roll, truck hunting and vertical bounce. Extreme cases of these dynamics can cause derailment.

Advice of Shipment. A notice sent to a local or foreign buyer that a shipment has gone forward, and containing details of packing, routing, etc.

Adzing Machine. Specially designed portable power-operated machine used to dress the rail seat on ties, thereby providing proper bearing for rail or tie plates.

A.E.R.A. The abbreviation for American Electric Railway Association.

Aeration. A cleaning and purification process involving the exposure of water to intimate contact with air for the oxidation of iron or organic matter, and for washing out gases and odors.

Aftercooler. A radiator unit for cooling compressed air after it has been heated by compression.

Agency Station. A station or depot where an agent is located. See Open Station.

Agency Tariff. A tariff issued by a selected person with power of attorney (and usually for two or more carriers); also called an agency issue.

Agreed Weight. A weight mutually decided upon by shipper and carrier for commodities transported in a particular container or package, or in a certain manner, when actual weights are not critical.

A.I.E.E. Abbreviation for American Institute of Electrical Engineers.

Air Arc (Welding). A metal cutting process wherein the severing of metal is effected by means of a chemical reaction of oxygen with the base metal at elevated temperatures, the necessary temperature being maintained by means of an arc between an electrode and the base metal.

Air Brake. The general term used to describe the braking system used on most railways operating in North America. See AB Brake.

Air Brake Hose. The flexible hose at each end of a car which is fastened to the brake pipe angle cock on one end, and has a fitting on the other end which engages with a similar coupling on an adjoining car. Sometimes known simply as "the air hose," or the "brake hose." See Trainline.

Air Brake Hose Coupling. A special type of standardized fitting which is attached to one end of an air brake hose in order to provide means for rapid and positive connection and disconnection of the hoses between adjacent cars.

Air Brake Hose Nipple. A short metal tube of standard A.A.R. design formed on one end for forcing into the end of standard air brake hose where it is held by a suitable clamp. The other end of the nipple is threaded, and screws into the angle cock.

Air Brake Instruction Car. A railway service car, usually a passenger train car, in which is installed the apparatus necessary to illustrate and explain the construction and operation of the air brake system and its parts. It is used for the instruction of train crews and other employees whose duties require knowledge of air brake operation and maintenance.

Air Buffer. An air cylinder with a piston valve which checks the escape of air when activated, thereby acting to lessen the shock of impact.

Air Cell. A small receptacle connected to an engine cylinder into which some of the compressed air is forced, and through which air later flows into the cylinder to complete combustion of unburned fuel.

Air Chamber. A closed chamber installed on the discharge or suction side of a pump to assist in achieving a uniform flow of water and to equalize stresses on the pump and the piping.

Air Compressor. A power-driven air pump which on locomotives and self-propelled cars supplies compressed air for the operation of air brakes and other air-actuated equipment. Compressors may be driven from the engine or by an electric motor, either directly or through V-belts and pulleys.

Air Compressor Governor. A device designed to automatically open or close the circuit to the electric motor driving the compressor, or in the case of a mechanically driven compressor, to unload the intake valve when the air pressure in the discharge line exceeds a predetermined limit, and again to start the operation of the compressor when the discharge air pressure falls below a predetermined limit.

Air Compressor Governor Synchronizing System. An arrangement for ensuring an equal division of work of furnishing compressed air for braking and other purposes, among all motor or mechanically driven air compressors in a train.

Air Condenser. A device used for removing moisture from compressed air by cooling the air.

Air Conditioning. Broadly, the simultaneous adjustment of atmospheric conditions, chemical as well as physical, within an enclosed space, to suit the requirements of the purpose for which that space is used, regardless of variations in natural atmospheric conditions. This process involves control of moisture content, temperature, purity, circulation, and sound.

Air Gage (Air Brake). A dial type pressure measuring device used to register the pressure of air in the reservoirs, brake pipe or brake cylinders. Duplex gages with two pointers are available for measuring two pressures on the same dial face.

Air Gage Fitting. A pipe connection by means of which an air gage is connected to the pipe or device containing the pressure that is to be measured.

Air Gap, Magnetic. Air space between two adjacent parts of a magnetic circuit before the application of a protective coating.

Air Gaps. The clearance between the armature core and the stationary field poles of a generator or motor.

Air Horn. A warning device designed for locomotive applications which emits a loud sound when compressed air is supplied through a manually operated valve.

Air Hose. See Air Brake Hose.

Air Injection. The system of injecting fuel into the combustion chamber of a diesel engine by means of a blast of highly compressed air.

Air-Inlet Ports. Openings through the cylinder liner of a two-cycle diesel engine, which are uncovered by the piston near its downward stroke, through which scavenging air and air for the next power stroke enters the cylinder. Exhaust may take place through ports at the opposite end of the cylinder in an opposed piston engine, or through exhaust valves in the cylinder head of a single-piston cylinder.

Air Intake Manifold. A conduit with lateral connections clamped to the air inlet opening in each cylinder head through which air from the scavenging blower or supercharger passes to the inlet valves ineach cylinder head. In some V-type engines it is formed by enclosing the "V" at the top of the cylinder block.

Air Pipe (Air Brake). More properly known as the brake pipe, and often called the "train line."

Air Signal. See Back-Up Air Signal and Train Air Signal.

Air Space (Refrigerator Cars). Space purposely left between linings or layers of insulation in floor, sides, and ends, to provide additional insulation. It is sometimes called "dead-air space" as distinguished from the ventilating air passages, as the air in the former is confined and not constantly changing.

Air Spring. An elastomeric unit inflated with low-pressure air used in the suspension system of transit cars or lightweight passenger cars.

Air Starter. A device used to start an internal combustion engine by admitting compressed air into the cylinders.

Ajax Diaphragm. A flexible fabric structure used to close off vestibules between passenger cars.

Alarm Circuits. Electrical circuits arranged to indicate faulty operation of any of the several systems which may be under an operator's control. Alarms may be indicated by bells, lights, or buzzers and protect lubricating oil, cooling water, fuel and other vital systems on a locomotive.

Alcove Lamp. An interior light recessed in the side of a passenger car.

Alerter. An electronic device to automatically cut off locomotive power and apply brakes in the event the locomotive engineer becomes incapacitated. See Deadman Control.

Align (Optics). Adjustment of the mounting of a lighting unit to direct its projected beam toward a specific object or area.

Alignment (Civil Engineering). A railroad's horizontal location as described by curves and tangents.

Alignment Control Couplers. Specially equipped couplers installed on some locomotives that will allow only limited lateral movement when in buff, and therefore reduce the possibility of rail turnover and jackknifing of the locomotive consist.

Alley (Noun). Clear track in switching yard.

Alloy Steel. Steel to which has been added silicon, manganese, nickel, or other elements to give greater strength, or to impart other desirable properties for a particular use.

All-Rail. An act of carriage entirely by rail transportation, but broad enough to include those lines or that service using car ferries or lighters.

Alternate Standard. A product or device which is approved by the A.A.R. to serve as an acceptable requirement for use in interchange service in lieu of the Standard, and is equal to or exceeds the requirements of the A.A.R. Standard. (A.A.R.)

Alternating Current. An electric current that reverses its direction at regular intervals.

Alternator. A device that generates alternating current electricity.

Alternator, Tuned. A direct current generator having contacts which operate to interrupt a direct current to produce a predetermined frequency by mechanically "tuning" its component parts, thereby producing alternating current.

Aluminum. A light, silvery, malleable, and ductile metallic element. When alloyed with other elements, aluminum is used in railway car construction.

Aluminum Alloys. Aluminum to which has been added various other elements to impart qualities suitable for a specific purpose. These alloys are available in the form of rolled or extruded structural shapes, castings, etc. for car construction.

Amfleet Cars. Passenger type, non-powered rail cars designed for Amtrak intercity service.

Ammeter. An instrument for measuring electric current in a circuit.

Ampere. The fundamental unit of measure for electric current. One ampere is defined as the current that flows when a potential of one volt is impressed on a resistance of one Ohm.

Ampere-hour. The quantity of electricity equivalent to a current of one ampere flowing past a point in a conductor in one hour. Sometimes simply called an "amp-hour."

Ampere Turns. A means for measuring the magnetizing power, or magneto-motive force developed by a current of electricity in a conducting coil. It equals the product of the number of turns in the coil multiplied by the current in amperes.

Anchor (Construction). A device used in connection with rods, wires, ropes, bolts, or other connecting supports, to give stability to the whole or part of a structure, or to secure it to a foundation.

Angle (Steel Structure). A general term applied to rolled steel structural members having an L-shaped cross section.

Angle Bar. One of two bars used to join two railends together to form continuous track.

Angle Cock. A special type of 1-1/4" valve of either ball or plug design, located at both ends of the brake pipe on locomotives and cars and used to control admission of air to the brake pipe on individual cars. The free end is angled at 45 degrees and is threaded to receive the air hose nipple.

Angle Cock Handle. The operating handle of the angle cock, having a self-locking feature to minimize the chance of accidental opening or closing of the valve.

Angle Fitting (Air Brake). A special pipe elbow for use with brake and signal pipe hose couplings.

Angle Globe Valve. A globe valve having the inlet and outlet connections at an angle with each other, commonly 90 degrees.

Annealing. A heat treating process whereby the temperature of an iron base alloy is raised and held above the transformation range for a time, followed by slow cooling, thereby equalizing internal stresses and increasing ductility.

Annunciator. A device for visual signaling, having a number of pilot lights, each of which indicates the status of an associated circuit and is labeled for circuit indentification. Annunciator panels are installed on modern locomotives.

Anode. The positive electrode by which current enters an electrolytic cell or storage battery when it is on discharge.

A.N.S.I. Abbreviation for American National Standards Institute.

Anthracene Oil. A coal tar distillate, distilling between 270 deg. and 400 deg. C. Sometimes called "green oil."

Anti-Checking Iron. A piece of steel strip sharpened on one edge and bent in various shapes, which is driven into the end of a tie to prevent checking and splitting. These devices are commonly called by the name of the shape in which they are bent, that is, C-iron, S-iron, and Z-iron.

Anti-Creeper. See Rail Anchor.

A.P.B. Abbreviation for absolute permissive block. A term used in transportation rule books to describe a specific section or length of track to which certain rules apply.

API Gravity. An arbitrary scale adopted by The American Petroleum Institute for measuirng the specific gravity of a liquid in "degrees". Degrees API = (141.5 / specific gravity) − 131.5.

Apparent Power. The product of the current in a circuit multiplied by the voltage impressed on the circuit. Sometimes called "EI" power

Application Circuit (Electro-Pneumatic Brake). An electric circuit maintained throughout the length of a train for controlling the application and release of air brakes.

Apportionment Distribution. A system of car distribution whereby rolling stock is distributed on a definitely fixed basis. The term is also used in connection with the distribution of tonnage on a competitive traffic among competing carriers.

Apportionment Sheets. Sheets on which interline revenue is apportioned, and from which reports to carriers are prepared.

Approach Locking. A time sensitive electrical locking system to prevent the movement of track switches in a given route after a train is committed to that route, while at the same time protecting that route from opposing or conflicting movements.

Approach Signal. A fixed signal used to govern the approach to another signal.

Approval Withdrawn. The status of a formerly approved design, product, device or facility which has been found to be no longer acceptable for use on or involving equipment in interchange service. When applicable, removal from interchange service may be required within prescribed time limits. (A.A.R.)

Approved. The status of an item of equipment, practice, or procedure, design, product, device or facility which has been reviewed by the AAR Mechanical Division and found to meet the applicable requirements of an AAR Specification, Standard, Alternate Standard, or Recommended Practice. (A.A.R.)

Apron. A waterfront railroad track on a bridge structure that connects the deck of a car ferry with the tracks on land, hinged at the shore end so that it is free to move vertically at the outboard end to accommodate varying elevations of the ferry.

APT. Abbreviation for "advanced passenger train."

A.R.A. Abbreviation for American Railway Association.

Arbitrary (Rates). A stipulated and unvarying amount over and above a rate between two points, used to make a through rate.

Arbitration Committee. A standing committee of the A.A.R. Mechanical Division whose duty it is to settle disputes arising between the members under the Rules of Interchange and to recommend changes, amendments or additions to the Rules of Interchange as may be thought advisable from the experience of the preceding years.

Arc (Electric). A luminous glow or bow of light formed when an electric circuit is opened between two electrodes or terminals. Heavy arcing is undesirable and is sometimes controlled or surpressed by a strong magnetic field.

Arch (Construction). A curved structural element that enables applied loads to be transmitted to rigid supports by direct compression, or by combining direct compression with bending, and generally producing inclined reactions at its supports.

Arc Weld. A welding process whereby coalescence is produced by heating with an electric arc, with or without the application of pressure, and with or without the use of filler metal.

A.R.E.A. Abbreviation for American Railway Engineering Association.

Armature. The rotating part of a direct current motor or generator. It consists of a laminated iron cylinder or core keyed to a shaft, in the slots of which are wound the armature coils of insulated copper wire or bars. In alternating current machinery the armature is frequently the stationary element.

Armature Spider (Electric Motor). A skeleton center fastened to the armature shaft and surrounded by the laminated iron core in which the armature coils are embedded.

Armored Cable. A cable with a protective covering, usually consisting of helically laid galvanized steel wires.

Armored Hose. Air brake or signal hose covered with woven wire fabric, or other heavy material to protect it from injury or abrasion.

Articulated Car. A car created by the uniting of two or more railcar segements or units to form a single unit whose joints are created by a drawbar or coupling included between the segements or units. Many articulated cars share a common truck under the articulated joints.

A.S.C.E. Abbreviation for American Society of Civil Engineers.

A.S.M.E. Abbreviation for American Society of Mechanical Engineers.

Aspect (of a Signal). The appearance of a fixed signal conveying an indication as viewed from the direction of an approaching train; the appearance of a cab signal conveying an indication as viewed by an observer in the cab.

Asphalt Cement. An asphaltic material that may be fluxed or unfluxed, especially prepared as to quality and consistency, used directly in the manufacture of asphaltic pavements, and having a penetratration of between 5 and 250.

Asphalts. Solid or semi-solid bitumens found either in a natural state, or obtained by refining petroleum, which melt when properly heated, and consist of a mixture of hydrocarbons and their derivatives.

Assigned Car. A railcar specifically designated for use of a particular shipper, or, in the case of private cars, for the use of a particular railroad for a specific service.

Assigned Siding. A side or team track owned by a carrier and assigned to one or several industrial concerns for loading or unloading.

Association of American Railroads. See A.A.R.

A.S.T.M. Abbreviation for American Society for Testing Materials.

Astray Freight. Less-than-carload freight which is marked for destination and which has become separated from the regular revenue waybill.

Atomization (of Fuel). The breaking up of fuel into a fine spray which mixes uniformly with the air as it enters the combustion chamber of a diesel engine.

Audible Cab Indicator. A device (usually an air whistle) located in the cab of a locomotive equipped with cab signals and designed to sound when the cab signal aspect changes and to continue sounding until acknowledged.

Auger. A wood-boring tool used for boring holes larger than can be made with a gimlet. The handle of an auger is attached at right angles to the tool line. There are several different types of augers made for various purposes.

Automatic. A term applied to any device designed to function without manual assistance, as distinguished from one in which the changes are made manually.

Automatic Air Brake. Pertaining to the air brake system used for stopping trains. See AB Brake.

Automatic Block Signal System. A block signal system where the use of each block is governed by an automatic block signal, cab signal, or both.

Automatic Circuit Breaker. A device designed to operate automatically to interrupt an electric circuit under predetermined conditions of load, temperature, or other criteria.

Automatic Clutch (Generator Drive). A self-acting device which engages the driving mechanism with the generator when the speed of the former becomes sufficient, and disengages the two when the driving speed falls below a predetermined value.

Automatic Coupler. See Coupler.

Automatic Double Acting Slack Adjuster. See Slack Adjuster.

Automatic Empty-And-Load Brake. A modified AB freight car brake in which a changeover valve, activated by a device on one of the trucks which measures spring deflection, directs air from the AB valve to one brake cylinder when the car is empty and two brake cylinder when the car is more than half loaded.

Automatic Interlocking. See Interlocking, Automatic.

Automatic Lubricator. A device for feeding at regular intervals a certain quantity of oil or lubricant to a mechanism requiring lubrication. See Lubricator.

Automatic Signal. A general term applying to any signal device that operates automatically.

Automatic Slack Adjuster. See Slack Adjuster.

Automatic Train Control System (ATC). A track-side system working in conjunction with equipment installed on the locomotive, so arranged that its operation will automatically result in the application of the air brakes to stop or control a train's speed at designated restrictions, should the engineer not respond. ATC usually works in conjunction with cab signals.

Automatic Train Operation (ATO). A system by which speed and other control signals from the wayside are automatically received and translated into train response with appropriate feedback to assure operating safety.

Automatic Train Stop System (ATS). A track side system working in conjunction with equipment installed on the locomotive, so arranged that its operation will result in the automatic application of the air brakes should the engineer not acknowledge a restrictive signal within 20 seconds of passing the signal. If the restrictive signal is acknowledged, ATS will be supressed.

Auto Parts Car. A boxcar specially fitted for transportation of automobile parts in racks without packing. Auto parts cars carry an A.A.R. mechanical designation of "XP".

Auto Rack Car. A flatcar with fixed steel racks, for transporting set-up automobiles. Racks have either two or three levels, and are equipped with tie-down devices. Auto rack cars carry an A.A.R. mechanical designation of "FA".

Auto-Railer. A self-propelled unit, powered by an internal combustion engine, equipped with alternative flange and pneumatic wheels, and thus suitable for both railway and highway operation.

Auto-Transformer. A transformer having only one coil which is tapped at intervals so that some of the turns may be used as a primary and some as a secondary winding to alter the ratio between the impressed voltage and the voltage delivered.

Auxiliaries. The term applied to a number of separately driven machines, operated by power from the main engine. They include the air compressor, radiator fan, traction motor blower, exciter for the main generator and the boiler blower. They are sometimes driven electrically and sometimes by mechanical means.

Auxiliary Brake Equalizing Lever (Six-Wheel Truck). A short lever to which the brake lever connecting rod is fastened, and which divides the power equally between the center pair of wheels and the outside pairs of wheels.

Auxiliary Drive. The mechanism of belts, shafts, gears or motors required to take power from the engine to the auxiliaries.

Auxiliary Fastenings. In track work, small parts such as tie plates, rail anchors, lock washers, rail braces, etc.

Auxiliary Generator. A generator provided to produce power for the various fuel, oil, and water pumps and to recharge the storage battery. This machine is generally driven by belts from the diesel or gears from the main generator. Passenger locomotives have an auxiliary generator for train lighting and sometimes heating.

Auxiliary Reservoir. A part of the air brake equipment on each railway car. Compressed air is stored in the auxiliary reservoir and is admitted to the brake cylinder to apply train brakes when brake pipe pressure is reduced. The auxiliary reservoir is isolated from the emergency reservoir by a separator plate bolted between the halves of the large reservoir tank on each car.

Average Haul. As applied to freight, the average distance in miles one ton is carried, computed by dividing the number of ton-miles by the number of tons carried, whether for an individual railway or for a group of railways, in either case representing the haul per railway. For the United States as a whole, it is also computed by dividing the total ton-miles by the tons of freight originated, thus giving effect to the fact that some freight originates on one railway and reaches its destination on another.

Average Load Per Car. The average number of tons of freight per loaded car obtained by dividing the number of tons originated (excluding LCL freight as the carloads of LCL freight are not separately reported) by the number of carloads originated. The term is also sometimes used to denote the average number of net ton-miles per loaded car-mile (including LCL freight) the miles of all loaded freight cars being used as divisor.

A.W.G. Abbreviation for American Wire Gage.

Axle. The steel shaft on which the car wheels are mounted. The axle holds the wheels to gage and transmits the load from the journal bearings to the wheels. See Black Collar Axle and Raised Wheel Seat Axle.

Axle Centering Machine. A machine used to cut the conical holes or lathe centers in the ends of axles.

Axle Collar. A rim or enlargement on the end of a car axle, which takes the end thrust of the journal bearing.

Axle Generator. A special type of electrical generator designed to be driven from the car axle by belt and pulleys or gear drive. Small axle generators for caboose power supply, for locomotive wheel slip control, etc., are driven from a connection with one end of an axle through a gear and splined shaft drive.

Axle Pulley. The belt pulley mounted on the car axle for driving an axle generator.

Axle Pulley Bushing. A bushing or sleeve, split longitudinally and bored conically inside to fit the tapering car axle and turned cylindrically outside to fit the hub of the axle pulley.

Axle Seat. The cylindrical surface of a car wheel which comes in contact with the axle (also called "the wheel bore"). The corresponding part of an axle is called "the wheel seat". Both surfaces are critical for a proper wheel fit on the axle.

Axle Spline Bushing. A steel cylinder pressed into the end of an axle at the axle center for driving control devices.

B

"B" End of Car. The end on which the hand brake is located. If the car has two hand brakes, the "B" end is the end toward which the body-mounted brake cylinder piston moves in the application of brakes. If the car has two hand brakes, the "B" end is the end on which the retaining valve is located (if such a valve is used). If none of the above definitions are applicable, the car owner shall arbitrarily designate the "B" end.

"B" Unit. A diesel unit without a cab and without complete operating controls. "B" units are usually equipped with hostler controls for independent operation at terminals, and engine houses.

Babbitt Metal. An alloy, consisting of tin, copper, and antimony, sometimes used for lining journal bearings. The term is commonly applied to any white alloy for bearings. Lead bearings are different in that they merely use a thin sheet of lead over the brass to correct slight irregularities and give an even bearing surface.

Back Contact. Part of an electric relay.

Back Cylinder Head (Air Brake Cylinder). See Non-Pressure Head.

Back Haul. To haul a shipment back over a part of a route which it has traveled.

Backhoe. An excavating machine which has a loading bucket in front which is drawn back toward the machine when in operation.

Back Light (Highway Crossing Signal). An auxiliary signal light used to beam a highway crossing signal in a direction opposite to that provided by the main unit.

Back-Up Air Signal. A warning whistle which can be operated from the rear of the train when backing up. Air for its operation is taken from the train line.

Back-Up Valve. A device, either portable or permanently installed, provided for the purpose of controlling brakes from the rear end of a train. It may have a whistle.

Badge Plate. A metal plate with stamped or engraved information about some significant aspect of the equipment to which it is attached.

Bad Order (Noun). A car which is in need of mechanical attention or repairs.

Bad Order (Verb). During car inspection activities, the act of designating a car as a bad order car. Bad order cars may usually be identified by a distinctive cardboard tag tacked to the route board on the car.

Bad Order Track. A track on which bad order cars are placed either for light running repairs or for subsequent movement to repair tracks

Bag-Staff. A receptacle for receiving the staff from an engineman in a train staff system.

Balance Speed. The equilibrium speed at which the drawbar force exerted by the locomotive is balanced by the train resistance resulting in a constant speed.

Ballast. Material selected for placement on the roadbed for the purpose of holding the track in line and at surface.

Ballast Car. A car for carrying ballast for repair and construction work, usually of either the flat, gondola, or hopper type.

Ballast Cleaning. The process of separating dirt from the ballast by shaking and depositing stone back onto the track.

Ballast Curb. A length of timber placed longitudinally along the outer edge of the floor on ballast deck bridges to retain the ballast.

Ballast Deck Bridge. A bridge with a solid floor provided with drains supporting a standard track with ballast.

Ballast Fork. Device used for the movement of rock ballast.

Ballast Leakage. The leakage of electric current from one rail of a track circuit to the other through the ballast, ties, etc.

Ballast Plow. A machine used to level ballast or move ballast from the track or to the shoulder of the track.

Ballast Regulator. A device that distributes equal amounts of ballast.

Ballast Section. A vertical cross section of the track from the subballast up, including ballast.

Ballast Spreader. A device used to evenly distribute ballast material on both sides of the track.

Ballast Sweeper. Also called a "broom." Cleans ballast off the track.

Ball Valve. So named because of a steel or brass ball which serves as its key operating part and opens to a full discharge rate with only a 90 degree turn of the handle. The ball has a passageway which permits flow of product through the valve if the passageway is in alignment with the valve opening. When the ball is rotated, the flow of product is cut off.

Banner. The actuated component of a disc or wig-wag signal.

Banquette. Supplemental embankment or shoulder on the land side of a levee for the purpose of preventing the line of saturation from reaching the surface of the levee slope, also to provide a break in the surface drainage.

Bar (Car Work). A long steel rod used for prying, lifting and other heavy work.

Bar (Civil Engineering). A shelving elevation of earth or sand which rises considerably above the adjacent area of the bottom of a waterway.

Bar, Locking. A bar in a signal interlocking machine to which the locking dogs are attached.

Base Adapter. See Adapter, Base.

Basic-Oxygen Steelmaking. This term is used generically to describe a process in which molten iron is refined to steel under a basic slag in a cylindrical furnace lined with basic refractories by directing a jet of high-purity gaseous oxygen onto the surface of the hot metal baths.

Batten In Car Doors The complete closing of the car doorway against rain, dust, snow, etc., by use of weather stripping and paper or plastic sheets.

Batter. A surface deformation of the head of the rail in the immediate vicinity of the end.

Batter Pile. A pile driven at an inclination to resist forces which are not vertical.

Battery. A group of cells connected together and capable of producing a direct electric current (DC) by chemical action when the positive and negative terminals are connected together through an electrical circuit. Common usage permits application of this designation also to a single cell used independently.

Battery Box. A container usually suspended from the underframe of passenger cars, locomotives, and cabooses. It houses the electric storage batteries used for car lighting, air conditioning, engine starting, etc.

Battery Charger. A device for restoring the electrical charge in a battery.

Battery-Charging Receptacle. A receptacle for charging a locomotive, car or caboose battery from an external source of power.

Battery Chute. A small cylindrical recepticle for housing track batteries and set in the ground below the frost line.

Battery Jar. A container for the solution and elements of a storage battery.

Bay Window Caboose. A caboose car having side bay windows instead of a cupola. This permits the train crew to look along the side of a train, especially when rounding curves, for detection of hot boxes or other trouble.

Bead. A small projecting molding of semi-circular section. Also, the strips on the sash frame which form a guide for the sash These beads are known as the "inside bead", "outside bead", and "parting bead".

Bead Weld. A type of weld characterized by the deposition of weld metal in a narrow unbroken string on the base metal.

Beam. A general term used in engineering construction that applies to the withstanding of bending stresses. In car construction the sills are fundamentally beams. Brake beams are part of the foundation brake apparatus.

Bearing. That which supports or on which something rests and is in contact. The metal block or bushing in contact with a journal is called a "bearing." See Journal Bearing, Rolling Bearing, Side Bearing.

Bearing Metal. An alloy of copper and tin or tin and zinc to which antimony and lead are sometimes added for use in engine and car journal bearings. See Babbitt Metal.

Bed Plate. The structure on which the engine frame is supported and which is bolted to the locomotive frame, of which the oil pan is an integral part.

Bell. A warning device on a locomotive or self-propelled car. It is usually bell-shaped and is equipped with a ringer which is operated by the engineman.

Bell Crank. A pivoted crank having two arms usually at right angles to each other and in the same plane for changing the direction of force 90 degrees, more or less. Bell cranks are used on freight cars in the hand brake system.

Belt. A band of flexible material, passing around two pulleys, communicating motion from one to the other. They may be flat or of "V" cross section, the latter usually being used in multiple.

Belt Line. A short line railroad operating within and/or around a city; usually organized to be a pickup, delivery and transfer service facility for trunk lines and industrial plants.

Belt Rail. A perforated structural angle attached to the interior sidewalls of a boxcar and used to locate and lock cross bars for providing lading restraint.

Bench Wall. The side wall or abutment of a culvert or tunnel.

Berm. The space between the top or toe of slope and excavation purposely made for intercepting ditches or borrow pits. An approximately horizontal space introduced in a slope.

Bessemer Process. A steelmaking process whereby liquid pig iron is converted to steel by forcing air at atmospheric temperature through the metallic bath in a converter in which no extraneous fuel is burned, resulting in the oxidation or reduction of the carbon, manganese and silicon to the extent desired and their removal in the form of slag.

Bethell Process. A process whereby wood receives full-cell pressure treatment with an oil preservative.

Bi-Level Car. A flat car designed with integral superstructure of posts, bracings and decking to permit loading of set up automobiles on two levels. In passenger car construction, design which places passengers on two levels through the length of the car.

Billet. In steelmaking, a semi-finished product which is either square or rectangular in section, and having a maximum cross-sectional area of 36 sq. in. and a minimum cross-sectional dimension of 1-1/2 in.

Billet Car. A low side gondola car built of steel throughout for transportation of steel billets or other heavy material.

Billing Card Holder. A holder for billing instructions generally mounted on the end platform or on the sides of the body bolsters.

Billing Repair Card. The card which, under A.A.R. Interchange Rules, is furnished to the car owner when repair work is done on a foreign car. The form and data contained on the card are specified in The Interchange Rules.

Bill of Lading. A carrier's contract and receipt for goods specifying that the carrier has received certain goods which it agrees to transport from one place to another, and to deliver to a designated person or assignee for such compensation and upon such conditions are specified therein. Ladings are designated "Straight" and "Order Specify."

Binding Post. An electrical terminal where connections can be made and secured.

Black Box. A generic term used to describe an unspecified device which performs a special function or in which known inputs produce known outputs in a fixed relationship.

Black-Collar Axle. An alternate standard design of freight car axle for plain bearings, referred to as the black collar design because of the black colored, or "as forged" collar at the inside edge of the wheel seat. This type of axle is no longer produced.

Blade, Semaphore. The extended part of a semaphore arm which shows the position of the arm. (I.C.C.)

Blanket Rate. See Group Rate.

Blanket Waybill. A waybill covering two or more consignments of freight. See Waybill.

Blind-End Car. A term applying to the end construction of baggage, express post or some passenger carrying cars having no external platform or vestibule.

Block. A length of track of defined limits, the use of which by trains and engines is governed by block signals, cab signals, or both. (Standard Code)

Blocking and Bracing (Procedures). Safety precautions in loading of rail shipments, which must be in accordance with regulations of the I.C.C., FRA and the A.A.R.

Blocking Device. A device that blocks a lever or any other mechanism so that it cannot be operated.

Block, Limit Signal. A fixed signal, or hand signal in the absence of a fixed signal, at the entrance of a block to govern use of that block.

Block, Permissive. A block in manual or controlled manual territory, which may permit a train, other than a passenger train, to follow a train, other than a passenger train, in the block.

Block Signal. A fixed signal at the entrance of a block to govern trains and engines entering and using that block. (Standard Code)

Block Signal System. A method of governing the movement of trains into or within one or more blocks by block signals or cab signals. (I.C.C.)

Block Station. A place from which manual block signals are displayed. (Standard Code)

Bloom (Steelmaking). A blooming mill's semi-finished product which has a cross-sectional area greater than 36 sq. in., the usual form being square or rectangular in cross-section and special forms being designated as round and shape blooms.

Blowdown. The act of letting water out of a boiler under pressure in order to reduce the concentration of dissolved and/or suspended solids.

Blower. A general term applied to a group of machines, the functions of which are to propel air for ventilation or cooling or other uses.

Blow-Out Coil. A coil incorporated in a contactor which creates a magnetic field across the arc at the moment the contact is opened. This field accelerates the movement of the arc which forms as the contacts open and serves to quench or extinguish the arc before it causes damage to the contacts.

Blue Flag. A blue signal (flag by day, light at night), displayed at one or both ends of an engine, car or train, indicating that workmen are under or about it; when thus protected, it must not be coupled or moved. Each class of workmen will display the blue signals and only these same workmen are authorized to remove them. Other equipment must not be placed on the same track so as to obstruct the view of the blue signals without first notifying the workmen.

Boarding Car. A car used as a place of lodging for workmen.

Body Bolster. The transverse members of the underframe over the trucks which transmit the load carried by the longitudinal sills to the trucks through the center plates.

Body Center Plate. A cast or forged steel plate riveted or welded to the body bolster at the car center line, the function of which is to transmit the body bolster load to the trucks through the truck bolster. See Truck Center Plate.

Body Side Bearing. A flat steel bearing pad fastened to the body bolster, a standard distance outboard from the center pin hole, the function of which is to support the load of a moving car when variations in track cross level or other train dynamics cause the track cross level or other train dynamics cause the car to rock transversely on the center plates. A conventional car has four body side bearings (one at each corner).

Bogie. The running gear of a highway semi-trailer which may be removable or longitudinally adjustable. Also, the European railway term applied to railway freight and passenger car trucks.

Bogus Plate (Refrigerator Cars). A horizontal member attached to the posts on the inside of the car, a short distance below the plate. The bogus plates support horizontal cross members called meat racks, or hanging bars, to which hooks are attached for hanging meat.

Bolster. See Body Bolster, Container Bolster, Truck Bolster.

Bolster Anchors. Rods, one at each end of the bolster of passenger car trucks, the ends of which are mounted in rubber, one on an arm integral with the truck frame and the other on the end of the bolster. The rubber mounting permits the rods to guide the lateral and vertical movement of the bolster. They position the bolster so that it is always free from contact with the truck transoms.

Bolster Center Filler. A box-shaped member placed between the center sill web plates and body bolster plates to reinforce the bolster at the center plate location.

Bolster Gibs. Small projections at each end of a truck bolster that engage the side frame column guides and provide vertical guidance for the bolster and lateral restraint to the side frames when assembled as a truck.

Bolster Hanger. See Swing Hanger.

Bolster Jack Screw (Wreck Cranes). A jack screw attached to the spring plank for the purpose of taking the load off the springs and making the entire truck and car body one rigid structure when the derrick of the crane is in use.

Bolster Roll Stabilizer. A device consisting of a separate spring plank on each side of the truck. These are connected across the truck by levers pivoted to the bolster and linked together at the center, thus transferring excess load on bolster springs at one side back to the other side and preventing the bolster from moving out of plane with the track.

Bolster Stiffener. A steel block or weldment placed between the webs of a body bolster, over the side bearings, to reinforce the bolster bottom cover plate, and provide for better distribution of the side bearing loads.

Bolster Top Cover Plate. In a fabricated body bolster, the heavy steel plate forming the top cover between the two vertical web plates.

Bolster Webs. In a fabricated body bolster, the vertical steel plates forming the filling pieces between the top and bottom cover plates.

Bond, Rail (Joint). A metallic connection attached to adjoining rails to insure electrical conductivity.

Bond Wire. The cable connecting the ends of adjoining cable.

Boom. A spar or beam projecting from the mast of a derrick, supporting or guiding the weights to be lifted.

Boom Car. A wreck train car using a derrick over which the derrick's boom rides.

Bootleg. A protection given to track wires where the wires leave the conduit or ground near the rail.

Borer, Penetrance. A hollow auger which as it turns, fills with a core of wood, which is extracted for determining the depth of penetration by a preservative or the width of the sapwood.

Borrow Pit. An excavation usually made near a trackwork site to obtain embankment material.

Bottom Rod. The brake rod connecting the bottom ends of the live and dead truck brake levers. The bottom rod is sometimes called the "bottom truck connection" or the "spreader." See Brake Rod.

Bottom Rod Safety Support. A device designed to support the bottom rod and to prevent it from dropping to the track in case of failure of any part which normally supports the bottom rod.

Boxcar. A closed car having a floor, sides, ends and a roof with doors in the sides, or sides and ends. Used for general service and especially for lading which must be protected from the weather.

Box Lid. See Journal Box Lid.

Box Section. A structural member, usually a weldment, whose cross-section is of rectangular shape.

Brace. An inclined piece which unites two or more of the points of a frame or truss, where other members of the structure are connected together and which prevents them from turning about their joints.

Bracing. Protection of the contents (lading) of a car from shifting and subsequent damage.

Braided Cable. A cable consisting of one or more insulated wires covered with a braided fabric.

Braiding. The interwoven covering of wires or cables.

Brake. The whole combination of parts by which the motion of the locomotive or train is retarded or arrested. The foundation brake gear includes all of the parts by which the pressure of the air in the brake cylinder is transmitted to the wheels. See AB Brake, Hand Brake.

Brake Application. The term used to describe the act of applying the brakes, generally accomplished by operating the automatic brake valve on a locomotive.

Brake Balancer. A modification in the foundation brake rigging whereby the top of the dead lever is connected to the car body instead of to the truck bolster. The object of the device is to relieve the truck from unbalanced stresses.

Brake Beam. The immediate supporting structure for the two brake heads and two brake shoes acting upon any given pair of wheels. In freight service the virtually universal type is of truss construction consisting primarily of tension and compression members fastened at the ends and separated at the middle by a strut or fulcrum to which the truck brake lever is attached. Brake beams are said to be inside hung or outside hung, according to whether they are in the space between the axles or outside the axles.

Brake Beam Hanger. A rod or bar by which a brake beam is hung or suspended from a truck. More commonly referred to as "brake hanger."

Brake Beam Safety Support. Usually a rigid angle or bar attached to the truck spring plank, passing underneath the beam, to prevent beams from falling to the track as in the case of broken beam hangers, etc.

Brake Beam Strut. The structural member between the tension and compression members of a brake beam; to it is attached the truck brake lever. Also called "brake lever fulcrum."

Brake Beam Supports. Cast integral slots in truck side frames for supporting the ends of the brake beam.

Brake Chain. The chain that connects the hand brake to the brake cylinder push rod.

Brake Chain Drum. The enlarged end of the hand brake shaft on which the chain is wound.

Brake Chain Sheave. An iron wheel or pulley around which the brake chain passes.

Brake Chain Worm (in Horizontal Wheel Hand Brake Systems). A conical casting attached to the brake shaft with a helical external groove for the brake chain. Its objective is to produce a rapid motion at first and increase the power when the brake shoes are brought to bear against the wheel.

Brake Clevis. A "U" shaped steel section with pin holes in each leg for making a connection between a brake rod and a brake lever.

Brake Connecting Rod. The rod (or rods) transmitting braking force from the cylinder levers to the truck live levers.

Brake Cylinder. A steel cylinder attached to the body frame or truck frame of a car or locomotive containing a piston which is forced outward by the compressed air to apply the brakes. When the air pressure is released, the piston is returned to its normal position by a release spring coiled about the piston rod inside the cylinder.

Brake Cylinder Lubricator. A device for supplying oil or grease to the brake cylinder.

Brake Cylinder Pipe (Car). The pipe that connects the brake cylinder to its operating valve. (Locomotive). The pipe that connects the distributing valve to all the brake cylinders in the locomotive brake equipment.

Brake Cylinder Plate. The steel plate to which a brake cylinder is bolted and by which it is attached to the sills when the brake cylinder is attached to the car body.

Brake Cylinder Release Valve. A valve inserted in the brake cylinder pipe and mounted on the pipe bracket of the freight brake control valve. Its function is to permit the release of brake cylinder pressure without depleting the auxiliary or emergency reservoirs and brake pipe pressure. The ABD valve incorporates this feature in the service portion. It is operated by pull rods from the side of the car.

Brake Equalizer. See Floating Lever.

Brake Hanger. A link or bar by which brake beams and attachments are suspended from a truck frame. It is attached to the truck by a brake hanger pin or carrier.

Brake Head. A casting attached to a brake beam which carries the detachable brake shoe.

Brake Head Adjusting Spring. A spring attached to the brake head for the purpose of holding the shoe in alignment and still allowing yield enough to permit automatic adjustment to the face of the wheel. Also called "balance spring."

Brake Hose. See Air Brake Hose.

Brake Lever. A general term designating the levers used as part of the foundation brake gear. See Dead Lever, Live Lever, Floating Lever, Cylinder Lever.

Brake Lever Badge Plate. Generally a small relief casting fastened to the car center sill, in schematic fashion certain truck and car body brake lever dimensions.

Brake Lever Bracket. A general term for any bracket which serves as a fulcrum for a brake lever. The bracket may be intergral with, or attached to either the car underframe or the truck frame or bolster.

Brake Lever Connection. A rod connecting two brake levers. Most commonly used to designate the rod connecting the lower ends of the truck brake levers.

Brake Lever Fulcrum. See Brake Beam Strut.

Brake Lever Guide. An elongated clevis the jaws of which guide the upper end of a brake lever. Further distinguished as "live lever" and "dead lever" guides, the latter provided with pins for readjustment as the brake shoes wear. Also called a "brake lever stop." See Dead Lever Guide.

Brakeman. A person who assists with train and yard operations.

Brake Pawl. A small specially shaped iron or steel piece, pivoted to engage the teeth of a brake ratchet wheel to prevent the wheel turning backward, and thus releasing the brakes.

Brake Pin. Any of a series of hardened steel pins of varying diameters inserted through holes in the brake levers, beams, fulcrum, rod clevises, or other points in a foundation brake system to provide for positive connection between the parts.

Brake Pin Cotter. A split pin inserted in a hole at the end of a brake pin to prevent it from working loose.

Brake Pipe. That section of the air brake piping of a car or locomotive which acts as a supply pipe for the reservoirs and also is usually the means by which the car brakes are controlled by the engineman. When a train is made up and all brake pipes on the cars are joined, the entire pipe line comprises what is commonly called the "train line."

Brake Pipe Air Strainer. On older cars, a strainer inserted in the brake pipe to prevent foreign matter from entering the brake apparatus under the car.

Brake Pipe Anchor. A device for holding the brake pipe in position.

Brake Ratchet. A wheel attached to the brake shaft having teeth which the pawl engages, thus preventing the wheel and shaft from turning backward.

Brake Regulator. A device designed to maintain the proper brake shoe clearance at all times. See Slack Adjuster.

Brake Rigging. The term applied to the entire system of levers, rods, fulcrums, brake beams and associated connections that serves to multiply the force created by air pressure in the brake cylinder and transmit it to the brake shoes. Rigging attached to the car underframe is commonly called the "foundation brake gear," and rigging attached to or supported by the trucks, is generally termed "truck rigging."

Brake Rod. Any of the rods which form the connections between brake levers and through which the braking force is transmitted.

Brake Rod Guide. A bracket attached to the car underframe as a support for a brake rod.

Brake Shaft. A shaft on which a chain is wound and by which the power of a hand brake is applied to the wheels.

Brake Shaft Arm. A lever fastened horizontally on top of the brake shaft for turning it and applying the brake. Sometimes used instead of a brake hand wheel.

Brake Shaft Bearing. A metal sleeve through which a brake shaft passes and in which it turns. Sometimes called a "brake shaft guide."

Brake Shaft Step. A bearing which holds the power end of a brake shaft. It usually consists of a U-shaped bar of iron, the upper ends of which are fastened to the car body with a hole in the bar which receives the end of the shaft. The brake shaft step should not be confused with a "brake step." The latter is a shelf on which the brakeman may step when applying brakes.

Brake Shoe. A block of friction material formed to fit the curved surface of the tread of a wheel, and riveted or otherwise bonded to a steel backing plate having provision for quick and positive securement to the brake head. Brakes on most conventional railway cars depend on the friction created by the brake shoe rubbing on the wheel tread during a brake application. Brake shoes can be made of cast iron or of a high friction composition material, but because of the differing friction characteristics, cast iron and composition shoes are not interchangeable.

Brake Shoe Key. A key or wedge by which a brake shoe is fastened to a brake head. It is inserted through a keyway in the face of the brake head and the lug on the brake shoe.

Brake Step. A platform located on the "B" end of a car below the hand brake to provide a place to stand while operating the brake.

Brake Valve. The valve in the locomotive which the engineer operates the brakes. The term is also often used to refer to the control valve on a car.

Brake Warning Alarm. A device which senses excessive braking grid amperage, energizes a brake warning light and warning buzzer on the throttle stand, and on newer units, cuts out dynamic brakes.

Braking Power. A term used to describe the ability of a car to stop during a brake application. Braking power is determined by the total brake rigging lever ratio and the type of brake shoes on a car; and is measured as the total net brake shoe force with brake cylinder pressure at 50 lbs. per sq. inch. There are established maximum and minimum limits on braking power, expressed as percentages of gross loaded rail weight (minimum), and empty car weight (maximum).

Branch Line. A secondary line of a railway, as distinguished from the main line.

Branch Pipe. The pipe connecting the brake pipe to the control valve in the AB equipment.

Branding. Markings hot rolled in raised figures and letters in the rail web to identify the weight of rail and section number, type of rail, kind of steel, name of manufacturer and mill, and year and month rolled.

Brass. An alloy of copper and zinc. Also a term commonly used to designate a "journal bearing."

Break Bulk. The act of unloading and distributing a portion or all of the lading in a car.

Bridge Beam. A portion of abridge structure receiving and transmitting vertical, transverse, or oblique stresses produced by externally applied loads, when supported at its end or at intermediate points and ends.

Bridge Plate. A hinged device affixed to a TOFC flatcar at the BR and AL corners used to span the gap between coupled cars to enable circus loading of trailers. Flatcars with 15" end of car cushioning require auxiliary bridge plates at the BL and AR corners to provide the additional spanning length necessary when coupled to standard draft gear cars.

Bridge Tie. A transverse timber member resting on the stringers and supporting the rails. Also a sawed tie usually preframed and of the size and length required for track on a bridge.

Broad Gage. A railway track gage more than 4 feet, 8-1/2 inches.

Bronze. An alloy composed of copper and tin, sometimes with addition of small quantities of other metals such as nickel, phosphorus and silicon.

Brunorized. A patented heat treatment for rails consisting essentially of normalizing the steel. Named in honor of John Brunner, Carnegie-Illinois Steel Corporation.

Brush. A conductor serving to maintain electrical contact between the stationary and rotary elements of an electronic motor or generator.

Brush Holder. A metal bracket or support attached to the frame of an electric motor or generator, but insulated from it, for holding one or more brushes.

Btu. Abbreviation for British Thermal Unit. A measure of heat.

Buckled Track. A major irregularity in track alinement which is caused by excessive compression in the rails. Usually is unsafe for the passage of a train.

Buff. A term used to describe compressive coupler forces. The opposite of draft.

Buffer. The apparatus applied to the platforms of passenger cars for the purpose of closing the space between adjoining cars. Equipped with a shock absorbing device similar to a draft gear, the buffer also helps to absorb the impacts incidental to coupling cars and, in addition, cushions and smooths out other minor shocks and vibrations which occur during train movement.

Buffer Plate (Passenger Equipment Cars). A steel plate fastened to the end of the buffer stems, which bears against the opposing plate of the next car of the train. The vestibule face plate is bolted or riveted to and carried by the buffer plate.

Builder's Plate. A metal plate, commonly fastened on each side of a locomotive, giving the name of the builder, the builder's number and date of manufacture.

Bulk Freight. Loose freight such as coal, sand, flour and grain handled in its natural state, and not packaged, or boxed in individual units.

Bulkhead. A vertical partition generally extending the full width of a car and usually used to restrain lading. The term is also used to describe the transverse partitions in a passenger car.

Bulkhead Car. A flatcar equipped with bulkheads at each end, generally integral with the car body, extending the full width of the car deck at each end, and used to provide longitudinal restraint for open top loads.

Bullet Train. Japanese high-speed locomotive.

Bull's Eye. A convex glass lens which is placed in front of a lamp to concentrate the light so as to make it more conspicuous for a signal.

Bumping Post. A post at the end of a track used to stop equipment.

Burnett Process. Full-cell pressure treatment of application of a salt preservative to wood.

Burrs. Jagged or rough metal edges remaining at the point of machining or cutting of a metallic substance.

Bushing. A hollow cylinder made of some special purpose material and generally pressed into a hole or other opening in a dissimilar material to form a bearing for another mating part.

Business Car. A term frequently applied to a car used by railway officials while traveling. Equipped with office and living accommodations for eating and sleeping.

Bus or Bus Bar. A metal rod or bar for conveying electric current.

Butt End. A term applied to the end of a jaw without tang or thread.

Butt Joint. A term used in railroad welding to describe a joint between two adjacent members lying approximately in the same plane. A weld connecting the two members forming a butt joint is known as a "butt weld."

By-Pass Valve. A valve which, either through manual control or automatically, will pass a gas or fluid through a direct route or an alternate route, as may become necessary in connection with the operation of the particular apparatus to which it is applied.

C

Cab. The space in a locomotive "A-Unit" or "MU" car containing the operating controls and providing shelter and seats for the engine crew.

Cab Handhold. A rod or handhold on the back of the cab to assist the men in mounting or getting off a locomotive.

Cab Heater. A space heater for the engineman's cab usually electric, but sometimes hot water or steam.

Cabin Car. A term sometimes applied to caboose cars.

Cable (Electrical). Either a stranded conductor (single-conductor cable) or a combination of conductors insulated from one another (multiple-conductor cable).

Cable Ducts. The conduits for carrying the heavier electric wires or cables.

Caboose. A car usually placed at the rear of a train which provides an office and quarters for the conductor and/or trainmen while in transit, and for carrying the various supplies, tools, etc., used in freight train operations. From the caboose, the crew is also able to observe the condition of the train and initiate measures to stop the train if unfavorable conditions arise. Sometimes called "Cabin Car," "Way Car," or "Van."

Caboose Track. A track on which cabooses are held in a yard.

Caboose Valve. A rotary application valve placed in the caboose so that either service or emergency applications of the train brakes on freight trains may be made from the rear end.

Cab Signal. A signal located in engineman's compartment or cab, indicating a condition affecting the movement of a train or engine and used in conjunction with interlocking signals and in conjunction with or in lieu of block signals. (Standard Code)

Cafe Car. A car used in passenger service having a kitchen, usually in the center; one end arranged as a dining room, the other end being fitted for other uses, such as a coach, lounge or smoking room.

Cam. A rotating piece, either non-circular or eccentric, used to convert the rotary into reciprocating motion. The offsets on a camshaft are also called "the cams."

Camber. A slight deviation from a straight line, either horizontal or vertical, resulting in an arc between two points on the line. Long cars have a slight positive (upward) camber built into the center and side sills to allow for deflection of the car under load.

Cambering Machine. A device for giving hot rails emerging from the rolls the curvature required to compensate for the unequal cooling of head and base, so they will be as nearly straight as possible when cold.

Cam Follower. The part of the valve operating mechanism which holds the cam roller and guides its direction of movement. It may be a rocker or crosshead (the latter when the motion is transmitted by push rod).

Camshaft. The steel shaft on which cams are mounted to operate other devices such as valves, when the shaft is rotated.

Candlepower. A measure of the intensity of light.

Cant (of a Rail). A rail's inward inclination effected by using inclined-surface tie plates.

Cantilever. A projecting beam or structure supported at only one end. Cantilever construction is commonly used to support railway signals.

Capacitance. That property of a system of conductors and dielectrics which permits the storage of electricity when potential differences exist between the conductors.

Capacitor (Condenser). A device, the primary purpose of which is to introduce capacitance into an electric circuit.

Capacity. As applied to a freight car, the nominal load in pounds or gallons which the car is designed to carry. These figures are stencilled on the car and are identified as "CAPY." Capacity is not to be confused with load limit, which is the maximum weight that can be loaded in a given car.

Capacity (of a Battery). The number of ampere hours which can be delivered by a cell under specified conditions as to temperature, rate of discharge and final voltage.

Cap-Stringer Strap. A piece of iron or steel in round, square, or structural shape, straight or bent, used to fasten stringers to a cap by means of horizontal bolts without the use of drift bolts.

Car Accounting. A detailed account of the movement of car equipment over a carrier's lines, which is used under the per diem rules in the settlement of debits and credits.

Car Body. The main or principal part in or on which the load is placed.

Carbon Electrode. An electrode used in arc welding consisting of a carbon or graphite rod with no filler metal.

Carbon Steel (for Plain Steel). Steel containing only the elements carbon, sulfur and silicon in addition to iron; the properties of which are due essentially to the percentage of carbon in the steel.

Car Days. An expression referring to the number of days a car owned by one railroad is on the line of another railroad.

Card Board. A small wooden board secured to the outside of a freight car for tacking cards containing instructions pertaining to the load or to the car.

Car Dumper. A device for rapidly unloading bulk materials from open top cars by physically turning the car upside down.

Standard blocking for cradles of car dumping machines has been adopted by the A.A.R.

Car Float. A flat-bottomed craft without power and equipped with tracks upon which cars are run from the land by means of a float bridge, to be transported across water.

Carline. Framing members which extend across the top of a car from one side to the other and support the roof.

Car Lining. Material used on the interior of a car to protect the shipment.

Carload. The quantity of freight required for the application of a carload rate; the least weight at which a shipment is handled as a carload (known as C.L. Minimum Weight).

Carload Freight. A tariff term denoting freight transported by a rail carrier at other than L.C.L. or any quantity rates.

Carload Rate. A rate given a carload quantity of freight. See Minimum Carload Weight.

Carman. A person who repairs and maintains railroad cars.

Car Mile. An operating term defined as one car, moved over one mile of track.

Car Number. A number given a car in conjunction with owner's initials as a means of identification.

Car Performance. A general term used to express the usefullness of a car or group of cars in terms of miles traveled, revenue earned, average miles per day, or other specified criteria.

Car Pooling. The combining of car equipment owned by two or more railroads or private car owners, with operational control of the cars assigned to a central agency. Pooling agreements establish the terms under which the revenue and expenses will be shared by the individual car owners.

Car Rental. An amount which is paid for the use of private cars by carriers or shippers.

Car Replacer. A device for getting a derailed truck back on the track. It usually consists of an inclined plane or a curved surface, by which the wheels are raised when the car is pulled, so that the flange of the outside wheel can ride upon and over the rail. Also called "rerailing frog," or simply a "rerailer."

Car Retarder. A braking device built into a railway track to reduce the speed of cars being switched over a hump. Power activated shoes press against the lower portions of the wheels and slow the car to a safe coupling speed.

Carrier Iron. See Coupler Carrier.

Car Seal. A security device consisting of a thin metal strip with a serial number embossed on its surface, inserted through small holes in boxcar door operating hardware and permanently secured in such a manner as to make it impossible to open the door without breaking the seal. Seals can also be used on tank car dome lids and hopper car unloading outlets.

Car Service. A term applicable to the general services of railroads with respect to car supply, distribution and handling; involving such matters as demurrage, interchange, per diem charges and settlements, private car line mileage statements and allowances.

Car Service Rules. Rules established by agreement between railroads governing interchange of cars. (A.A.R.)

Casing. Any housing surrounding a piece of apparatus or machinery to protect it from damage.

Casting (Noun). A general term applied to any part or component made in a mold.

Casting. The disposal of excavated material by a single operation done either by hand or machinery.

Cast Iron. Alloys of iron containing 1.7 percent to 4.5 percent carbon, as cast, and usually not appreciably malleable at any temperature.

Cast Steel Wheel. A railway wheel made by pouring molten steel into a mold under well controlled conditions, followed by appropriate cleaning and heat treating. See Wrought Steel Wheel.

Catch Up. A colloquial expression applied to classification yards. It pertains to the situation where a car or cut of cars descending a grade from the apex of the hump overtakes a car or cut of cars before the one ahead has cleared the detector track circuit at a switch.

Catenary. On electric railroads, the term describing the overhead conductor that is contacted by the pantograph or trolley, and its support structure.

Cathode. The electrode by which electric current leaves an electrolytic cell when it is on discharge.

Caulking. Securing a rivet tightly by driving the edge of its head into surface of another piece; the act of sealing a joint or a seam with any caulking material.

C-Clamp. A temporary holding fixture used in metal fabrication work to secure components while welding, forming or machining. The device consists of a steel frame shaped roughly like a square letter "C", with an adjustable screw-operated clamp extending across the opening of the frame.

Ceiling Pressure. Generally used in conjunction with automatic schemes of car retarder control, pertaining to a limit placed upon maximum force exerted upon wheels of a car in a retarder for the purpose of preventing a "squeeze-out."

Cell. A general term pertaining to the elements of a storage battery along with its electrolyte and container.

Cement. A material of one of two classes, Portland and natural, the property of which causes hardening into a solid mass after being mixed with water.

Center Anchor (on Tank Cars). An arrangement of plates which are riveted to the tank and the center sills at the center of the car. These plates anchor the tank to the frame and supplant head blocks and double anchors at the ends.

Center Bearing. A term used to describe the interface or bearing between the truck and body center plates, as distinguished from the side bearings.

Center Bearing Bridge (Six-Wheel Trucks). A structure formed by the top and bottom center bearing arch bars to support the center plate block or center bearing beam and transmit the weight of the car to the bolsters on which its extremities rest.

Center Bolster (Six-Wheel Truck). A center bearing bridge made in a single unit of either built-up, welded or cast steel.

Center Draft Drawbar. A drawbar which is connected directly with the king bolt of a truck. It is especially designed for use on very sharp curves. Sometimes termed "radial drawgear."

Center Dump Car. A car which will discharge its entire load between the rails, often used in ballast service.

Center Frogs. The two frogs at the opposite ends of the short diagonal of a crossing.

Centering. Also called "centers"; a temporary support used in arch construction.

Centering Gage. A gage to locate the middle point of an axle, used in wheel-mounting operations.

Center Line. In drafting, a line passing through and defining the center of the object being depicted. Center lines are used as reference lines from which measurements are taken to locate other points.

Center Pin. The large steel pin which passes through the center of both the body and truck center plates and assists in keeping the two plates in proper alignment.

Center Plate. See Body Center Plate and Truck Center Plate.

Center Plate Block. The member supporting the center plate of a six-wheel truck.

Center Plate Centering Stud. A bar connecting the centering spring for the truck on some electric locomotives with the center plate serving to communicate the spring pressure to it and thus bring the center plate back to the central position after it has been displaced for any reason.

Center Sill. The main longitudinal structural member of a car underframe, often constructed as a large box section or hat section. The center sill receives all of the buff and draft forces created in train handling and switching.

Center Sill Bottom Flange. That portion of the center sill bottom cover plate extending outside of the webs on either side.

Center Sill Cover Plate. A heavy flat steel plate riveted or welded across the center sill webs either above (top cover plate) or below (bottom cover plate) or both, to form the sill.

Center Sill Separator. A filler piece placed between the center sill webs to maintain proper alignment and provide reinforcement for the webs at crossmember locations.

Center Sill Stiffener. A filling piece between the center sill webs to act as a brace for holding them rigid.

Center Sill Web. One of two vertical plates forming the sides of the box section center sill. The webs are connected by a top and/or bottom cover plate and a series of separators to maintain the proper spacing.

Central Bearing. A Commonwealth modification of the car body and truck center plates whereby the load is carried on a large concentric area 2 ft. in diameter which surrounds the center plate proper. The bearing surfaces are separated by a 1 in. thermoid pad. The bearing stabilizes the truck against hunting and performs the function of side bearings as well as center plates.

Centralized Traffic Control. A term applied to a system of railroad operation by means of which the movement of trains over routes and through blocks on a designated section of track or tracks is directed by signals controlled from a designated central point.

Centrifugal Dirt Collector. A device connected in the branch pipe between the brake pipe and control valve and so constructed that due to the combined action of centrifugal force and gravity, dirt and foreign material are automatically eliminated from the air flowing through the collector chamber and by means of a plug may be removed without breaking any pipe connections whatsoever. When this device is used, the brake pipe air strainer is omitted.

Centrifugal Pump. A circular casing within which revolves an impeller mounted on a shaft. The fluid enters the impeller at the center and passes outward between the vanes into the surrounding casing and to the discharge pipe.

Changeover Valve. A valve used with double-capacity brakes to enable changing from "empty" to "load" brake.

Changer Pole. A device by which the direction of current flow in an electrical circuit may be changed. (I.C.C.)

Channel. A commercial rolled steel bar shaped like a trough or channel. Channel sections are extensively used in railway car construction, particularly in the underframe.

Channel Pin. A tapered metal plug with one or two grooves used to fasten one or two bond wires to a rail.

Charge. In steelmaking, the raw materials placed in the furnace.

Charge. In wood treating operations, the total amount of wood assembled for treatment in one cylinder at one time.

Charge. In electric storage batteries, the restoration of the active materials in a battery by passing a unidirectional current through it in the opposite direction to that of the discharge.

Charging (Air Brake). A term used to describe the process of supplying the initial volume of compressed air to the air brake system on a car or train. A car is said to be fully charged when the brake pipe reaches and holds a pressure of 70 psi.

Charging Plug. An electric fitting or connection used to charge batteries.

Charging Rate. The current, in amperes, used to charge a storage battery.

Charging Receptacle. An electric fitting or connection device allowing for a plug-in connection to charge batteries on cars or locomotives.

Check Valve. Generally defined as a valve which permits flow in one direction only.

Cheek Plate. A casting which takes the place of draft lugs when horizontal coupler yokes and two key draft gears are used. See Draft Lug.

Chime. The rim around the base of a wooden water tank, formed by the stave-ends extending below the bottom of the floor.

Choke Coil. A form of stationary induction apparatus to supply reactance and used commonly in connection with signal lightning arresters.

Choke Fitting (Air Brake). A special pipe fitting with a restricted air passage to control the flow of air. Chokes are used in car and locomotive brake control valves and in various other parts of air brake equipment.

Chopper. A system used to provide variable D.C. voltage from a fixed D.C. voltage supply by interrupting the supply voltage in a controlled manner.

Chord (Car Construction). The long horizontal members at the top and bottom of a car side or end.

Circuit (Electrical). A complete path of an electric current including the generating device.

Circuit Breaker. A device for automatically opening an electric circuit when the current exceeds a predetermined amount.

Circus Loading. A term used to describe an older method of loading highway trailers on TOFC (piggyback) flatcars, whereby a tractor backs the trailer up a ramp placed at one end of a cut of cars, and along the decks of the cars to the point of securement. Circus loading requires bridge plates at each end of all cars to enable the trailer and tractor to pass from car to car. See Side Loading, Overhead Loading.

Claim. In shipping parlance, a formal demand made upon a carrier for the reimbursement for a loss, damage or over-charge. See such types as "Damage," "Loss," "Overcharge," "Relief," and "Reparation."

Claimant. One who makes a claim or demand.

Claim Tracer. A request for information relative to the status of a claim.

Clasp Brake. A truck brake rigging arrangement using two brake shoes on each wheel instead of the usual one. The shoes are on either side of the wheel and act in opposite directions like the jaws of a vice. Clasp brakes are used on locomotives and some iron ore cars, and in other applications where braking requirements are unusually heavy.

Class and Commodity Tariff. A schedule containing both class and commodity rates; generally with provision for their alternative application.

Classes (Shipping). The various divisions or groups designated by numbers, or by numbers and letters, into which articles offered for shipment are classified and to which rate schedules are adjusted.

Classification Track. One of the tracks in a classification yard, or a track used for classification purposes.

Classification Light. A light on a locomotive or car used to designate the class of the train.

Classification Yard. A rail yard consisting of an number of usually parallel tracks, used for making-up trains.

Claw Bar. A special steel tool about 5 feet long with a claw end and long shank lever designed to draw track spikes from railroad crossties by leverage. Often called a "spike puller."

Claw Jack. A jack having a step or projection at the bottom of the movable column, used when a bearing close to the ground is required.

Clearance. A general term meaning space between two objects.

Clearance Car. A special car equipped with a means of measuring and recording the maximum clearance through tunnels and past other structures along the right of way of the railroad. Data from the clearance car is used to determine the maximum height and width of equipment that can operate over individual segments of the railroad.

Clearance Diagram. An outline or cross section drawing representing the maximum limiting dimensions to which rail equipment can be built. Specific limiting dimensions have been established and are shown on standard clearance diagrams known as "plates."

Clearance Point. The location on a turnout at which the carrier's specified clearance is provided between the tracks. (I.C.C.)

Clearance Volume (Internal Combustion Engine). The volume of air space remaining in the cylinder when the piston has reached the end of its inward or compression stroke.

Clear Block. A block not occupied. Sometimes used to denote a clear signal indication.

Clearing Circuit. A term applied to a circuit used in connection with the operation of a signal in advance of an approaching train.

Clevis. A stirrup-shaped metal strap used in conjunction with a pin for attachment to the apparatus of which it is a part. Clevises are used extensively in brake rigging to connect the rods and levers.

Clip. In general, a device permanently attached to one part, whose function it is to hold another part in place, but with provision for easy removal.

Closed Circuit. A circuit is said to be "closed" when it is completed and current is flowing, as opposed to "open" when no current is flowing.

Closed Circuit Principle. The principle of circuit design where a normally energized electric circuit which, on being interrupted or de-energized, will cause the controlled function to assume its most restrictive condition. (I.C.C.)

Closed Car. Any roofed or permanently covered railway freight car, other than a tank car, used by a rail carrier for the transportation of freight by rail, as distinguished from "open top car."

Close Return Bend. A short cast tube made in a U-shape, for uniting the ends of two parallel pipes. It differs from an open return bend in having the two branches close to each other.

Closure Rails. The rails located between the parts of any special trackwork layout, as the rails between the switch and the frog in a turnout (sometimes called the Lead Rails or Connecting Rails); also the rails connecting the frogs of a crossing or of adjacent crossings, but not forming parts thereof.

Club Car. A term applied to a special type of parlor or lounge car, often arranged in two or more compartments and generally having movable instead of fixed seats. Where provided with a bar, such a car is also called a Tavern or Tap Room Car.

Clutch. A device installed in a rotating drive system to allow for partial or complete disengagement of the driving mechanism to meet varying demands of service.

Coach. A passenger carrying car, usually with a center aisle and two rows of twin seats..

Coach Yard. A yard in which passenger train cars are assembled, classified and/or prepared for service.

Coal Car. Usually a hopper or gondola car, for carrying coal.

Cobble. A piece of steel bent or twisted beyond the possibility of being finished by rolling.

Code (Rules). A general term used to describe any set of regulations dealing with some specific subject, such as interchange of freight cars or per diem.

Coded Track Circuit. A track circuit in which the electrical energy is varied or interrupted periodically.

Code Transmitter. A device to vary periodically an electrical circuit at a definite predetermined code frequency.

COFC. An acronym for "Container On Flat Car." A type of rail-freight service involving the movement of closed containers on special flat cars equipped for rapid and positive securement of the containers using special pedestals or bolsters.

Coil Gap (Tank Car Heaters). An undesirable condition caused by the spacing of heater coils too far apart to produce optimum thermal efficiency.

Coil Overlap (Tank Car Heaters). An undesirable condition, opposite of coil gap, in which the coils are spaced closer than necessary, thus creating an inefficient pattern of heating.

Coil Spring. A spring made by winding round wire or rods in a helical pattern around a circular core. Coil springs are used extensively in rail car suspension systems.

Coils (Tank Cars). A general term used to describe various types of heater pipe systems for tank cars. See Heater Pipes.

Coke Car. A car of large cubic capacity for carrying coke; usually a modified hopper car with doors which discharge the load to one or both sides of the track.

Coke Rack. A slatted frame or box, applied above the sides and ends of gondola or hopper cars, to increase the cubic capacity for the purpose of carrying coke or other freight, the bulk of which is large relative to its weight.

Cold Shot. Small globules of iron, resembling ordinary gun shot, which are found in castings. Cold shot defects are caused during the pouring operations by spatterings of iron sticking to portions of the mold where they cooled before being surrounded by the main mass of molten metal.

Cold Shut. A casting defect that occurs during casting of molten metal which may result from splashing, surging, or interrupted pouring. Cold shuts may be attributed to any factor that will prevent a perfect union where two surfaces meet and should fuse and blend.

Collar. A circular ring or flange usually at the end of a round shaft, and used for retaining some other part on the shaft.

Color Light Signal. A fixed signal in which the indications are given by the color of a light only.

Color Position Light Signal. A fixed signal in which the indications are given by color and the position of two or more lights.

Combination Rates. Two or more rates added together to make a through rate from a point of origin to destination. For example: the rate from New York to Omaha, Nebr., made on the Mississippi River combination, uses the rate from New York to the river as one factor and from the river to Omaha as the other.

Combination Station. A station where some of the station tracks are connected at one end only and some of the tracks are connected at both ends. See Stub Station, Through Station.

Combustion Chamber (Internal Combustion Engines). The clearance volume above the piston at the upper end of its travel. In a diesel engine the fuel is injected into this volume.

Commodity. A general term used to describe the contents of a car. Other terms such as "lading," "product" or "grade" mean the same thing and are often used interchangeably.

Commodity Stencilling. Lettering placed on the sides of any rail car describing any special ladings for which the car has been made suitable to transport.

Common Carrier. One who holds himself out to the general public to transport property and passengers, intrastate, interstate or in foreign commerce, for compensation. Common carriers must operate from one point to another over routes or in territory prescribed by the Interstate Commerce Commission (interstate) and by a Public Service or Public Utilities Commission (intrastate). See Contract Carrier.

Commutating Pole Motor. A railway motor in which four auxiliary coils and pole pieces called commutating poles are mounted between the four main field poles. The windings of these poles are connected in series with each other and with the armature. The commutation is improved and the poles perform their functions equally well regardless of the direction in which the motor is run. See Armature.

Commutation Fare. Carrier's charge (special rates) for traveling to and from suburban areas regularly, by week, month, etc., fare being less than one-trip rate.

Commutator. A cylindrical ring or disk assembly of conducting members, individually insulated in a supporting structure with an exposed surface for contact with current collecting brushes.

Company Car. In a general sense, a freight car owned by the carrier over whose line it is being operated as opposed to a "foreign car." Sometimes called a "system car."

Company Material. Material transported by a particular railroad such as rail, crossties, ballast, fuel oil, etc., used in connection with its operations.

Comparative Rate Schedule. A table of rates showing the differences in charges existing, if any, via two or more routes or via two or more of the several forms of carriage-rail, water motor carrier, etc.

Compartment. In passenger train service, a subdivision of a parlor or sleeping car running only partially across, allowing room for a corridor at the side. Sometimes called "stateroom."

Compartment Tank Car. A tank car in which the tank is divided into several sections for the purpose of carrying different commodities or smaller shipments.

Compensator. A device for counteracting the expansion and contraction caused by changes of temperature in a pipe line, thereby maintaining a constant length of line between units.

Composite Column. A circumferentially reinforced concrete column having a core of structural steel or cast iron, with each reinforcing element designed to carry a portion of the load.

Composite Construction (Freight Cars). A car with a combination steel and wood superstructure.

Compound Curve. Where two or more contiguous simple curves of different degrees provide a continuous change in the direction of alignment while having a common tangent at their junction points.

Compound Fissure (in a Rail). A progressive fracture starting from a horizontal split head which turns up or down in the head of the rail, continuing until substantially at right angles to the length of the rail. Compound fissures require inspection of both faces of the fracture to locate the horizontal split head from which they originate.

Compression. A general term used to describe forces which have a tendency to squeeze together.

Compression Ignition. Ignition of a fuel charge by the heat of the air in a cylinder generated by compression of the air.

Compression Member. Any part of a structure or truss that experiences compressive forces when serving its intended purpose.

Compression of a Train. The bunching of cars in a train caused by run-in of slack from the rear end.

Compression Ratio (Internal Combustion Engines). The ratio of the final pressure reached during compression to the pressure at the beginning of compression.

Compression Rings. Piston rings placed in the upper section of the piston barrel to seal against loss of compression and gas blowing.

Compressive Strength. The maximum compressive stress which a material is capable of sustaining without permanent deformation.

Compressor Cradle (Air Brake). A steel frame for supporting a motor-driven air compressor. The cradle is secured by means of brackets having pockets in which are rubber cushions so arranged as to prevent vibrations of the compressor from being communicated to the body and to allow its removal quickly and easily.

Compressor Synchronizing System. An arrangement of trainlined wires, relays, and pressure switches designed to equalize the load on a series of air compressors by causing all of them to "load" and "unload" simultaneously.

Compromise Joint (Trackwork). A rail joint between rails of different height and section, or rails of the same section but of different joint drillings.

Compromise Rail (Trackwork). A rail of relatively short length, the ends of which are of different section (see Rail Section), corresponding with the sections of the rails to which they are to be joined. A compromise rail eliminates the need for direct joining of rails of different section.

Computer Program (General). A plan or routine for solving a problem on a computer.

Concealed Loss or Damage. Loss or damage that cannot be determined until the package or carton is opened.

Concourse. In a large passenger station, a large gathering room used as a general passageway between the main waiting room and train shed.

Condenser (Electrical). See Capacitor.

Condenser (Air Brake). A device used for removing moisture from compressed air by cooling the air.

Conditionally Approved. The status of a practice or procedure, an item of equipment, a design, product, device or facility which has been reviewed by the AAR Mechanical Division and found to meet the applicable requirements for use in interchange service with restrictions imposed as to quantity, period of service, type of application, test conditions, or other limitations as stated in the applicable Standard, Specification or Alternate Standard. This term is used in lieu of former status "Approved for Test." (A.A.R.)

Conductivity. The relative facility with which a conductor transmits electric current. The term resistance is applied to the inverse or reciprocal of this property. Also called "conductance."

Conductor (Electrical). Electrical wire or cable that carries electric current.

Conductor (Train Operations). The individual in charge of the train crew.

Conductor's Valve. An air brake valve that can be operated from a car vestibule on the caboose.

Conduit. A passageway for electric conductors.

Conflicting Movements. Train movements over conflicting routes.

Conflicting Routes. Two or more routes, opposing, converging, or intersecting, over which movements cannot be made simultaneously without possibility of collision. (I.C.C.)

Connecting Rod. The rod which connects the crank and the piston.

Connecting Track. Two turnouts with the track between the frogs arranged to form a continuous passage between one track and another intersecting or oblique track or another remote parallel track.

Connector. A device for connecting the ends of two or more conductors.

Consistency (Construction). Descriptive of the state of fluidity of a mixture, embracing the entire range of fluidity from the driest to the wettest possible mixtures. The standard slump test is used to measure the consistency of freshly mixed concrete.

Construction Station (Trackwork). A 100-ft. distance as measured along the center line and designated by a stake bearing its number.

Contact. A conducting part which co-acts with another conducting part to open or close an electric circuit.

Contactor. An air or electrically-operated switch used to make or brake an electrical circuit.

Container. An independent structural unit, either open or fully enlcosed, designed for the intermodal transport of commodities. A large percentage of intermodal containers are designed with standard corner fittings for positive securement to highway trailers, rail cars or ocean-going vessels, thereby facilitating interchange between carriers in international trade.

Container Bolster. A container securement device generally used on raised center sill cars. Container bolsters are arranged to mount transversely on a flatcar, and support the container at each end.

Container Car. A car equipped to transport one or more removable containers.

Containerization. A term used to describe the hauling of freight in containers without wheels.

Container Pedestal. A securement device mounted on the deck of a flat car arranged to support a container at its corner fitting. Some COFC cars are equipped with adjustable pedestals for handling containers of various lengths.

Continuous Control. A type of locomotive control in which the locomotive apparatus is constantly in contact with the track elements, and is immediately responsive to a change of conditions in the controlling section which affects train movement.

Continuous Tractive Effort. That tractive effort that can be sustained indefinately by a locomotive without overheating any part of the locomotive traction equipment.

Continuous Welded Rail (CWR). Rails welded together in lengths of 400 or more feet. See Welded Rail.

Contract Carrier. See Common Carrier.

Control (Traction). A means of transmitting the desired engine output to the driving wheels in forward or backward operation.

Control Circuit. A low-voltage circuit which operates the contactors in a high voltage power circuit through relays and interlocks.

Controlled Manual Block System. A series of consecutive blocks governed by block signals, controlled by continuous track circuits, operated manually upon information by telegraph, telephone or other means of communication, and so constructed as to require the cooperation of the signalmen at both ends of the block to display a "clear" or a "permissive" block signal.

Controlled Point. A location where signals or other functions of both a traffic control system are controlled from the control machine. (I.C.C.)

Controlled Siding. A siding whose use is governed by signals under the control of a train dispatcher or operator.

Controller. The equipment at the engineman's position used to control the operation of a locomotive or M-U car.

Controlling Section. One or more track circuit sections governing approach to or movement within a block.

Control, Remote. A term denoting the control of any apparatus from a location apart from the location of the apparatus.

Control Stand. The upright column upon which the throttle control, reverser handle, transition lever, and dynamic braking control are mounted within convenient reach of the engineer on a locomotive. The air gages and some control switches are also included on the control stand.

Control Unit. In multiple unit locomotive consists, the locomotive unit from which the engineer operates the consist. Also called the "lead unit."

Control Valve. That part of the freight car air brake equipment on each car that controls the charging, application, and release of the brakes on the car. The three common types of control valves in use on modern freight cars are the AB valve, ABD valve, and the ABDW valve.

Conventional Sign. A symbol, which may be a mark, character, abbreviation or letter, selected or sanctioned by general agreement or common use to designate upon map or plan certain forms, conditionsor objects, both manual and structural.

Converter, Rotary. An electric machine having a commutator at one end and slip rings at the other end of the armature. It is used for conversion of alternating to direct current.

Convertible Car. A car so built that it may be converted without reconstruction from one type to another, as center-dump gondola (effective as a ballast car) to side-dump gondola (used as a car for grading).

Conveyor Car. A freight car equipped with motors for moving freight under special conditions, as on a coal wharf.

Cooling Coil. A coil or length of pipe carrying a refrigerant and having sufficient radiating surface to cool the surrounding fluid to a desired temperature. In air conditioning systems, the cooling coil is called the "evaporator."

Cooling Water. The fluid which circulates through the jacket space of cylinders and cylinder heads to prevent excessive heating of the castings.

Cooling Water System. The entire system of pumps, pipes, radiators, fans, and other apparatus installed on an internal combustion engine to cool the engine.

Core Loss. A term applied to the energy lost by hysteresis or eddy currents in the core of an armature, transformer or similar device.

Core (Magnetic). A mass of iron on which are placed magnetizing coils of an electromagnet.

Corner Brace. A diagonal member in the underframe between the end sill and transverse floor member or bolster. See End Sill Diagonal Brace.

Corner Casting. On freight cars, a heavy metal casting fitting on either the lower or upper outside corners of cars at the three-way joint formed by the two horizontal members and the vertical corner post for the purpose of reinforcing the corner joint. On containers, a standard casting that fits over all (8) corners of the unit and has holes for engaging standard securement locks on rail cars, trucks and ships.

Corner Post. The vertical member which forms the corner of the frame of a car body.

Corrosion. The deterioration or eating away of the surface of metal through chemical action.

Corrugated Rail. A condition of roughness on the rail head seen as alternate ridges and grooves, which develops in service.

Cost of Reproduction, New. As applied to Interstate Commerce Commission valuation, the estimated cost of reproducing the property of a carrier, based on the unit prices or price trends of a specific period.

COT&S An acronym for the periodic servicing of brake system components and indicating "Clean, Oil, Test and Stencil."

Cotter Pin. A slit pin inserted in a small hole and expanded to prevent its backing out. Used in place of a nut or to prevent a nut from becoming loose. See Brake Pin Cotter.

Counter Balances. Metal applied to the crank checks opposite to the crank pins on an engine crankshaft to balance the reciprocating forces produced by the piston and connection rod.

Counterbore. An enlargement, for a certain portion of its depth, of a smaller hole bored in any piece of material. The counterbore is made of sufficient depth to allow the head or the nut to come below the surface of the piece.

Countersink. To ream a hole to receive the conical head of a rivet, bolt, or screw so that the head will not project beyond the surface of the part connected.

Counterweight. Any weight applied to an apparatus for the purpose of balancing usually heavy forces that would otherwise hinder convenient operation of the apparatus.

Coupler. A device located at both ends of all cars and locomotives in a standard location to provide a means for connecting one rail vehicle to another. The standard A.A.R. coupler uses a pivoting knuckle and an internal mechanism that automatically locks when the knuckle is pushed closed, either manually or by a mating coupler. A manual operation is necessary to uncouple two cars whose couplers are locked together. See E Coupler, F Coupler and Shelf Coupler.

Coupler Butt. The extreme rear portion of the shank of a coupler.

Coupler Carrier. A casting or weldment, usually integral with the car end sill, serving to support the weight of the coupler while allowing it to pivot about its yoke connecting pin. Some coupler carriers are spring-mounted to allow for vertical movement of the shank when coupler head design restricts relative vertical movement between coupler knuckles.

Coupler Centering Device. An arrangement for maintaining the coupler nominally in the center line of draft but allowing it to move to either side when a car is rounding a curve while coupled to another car.

Coupler Contour. The shape or configuration of a coupler as it would appear traced on a horizontal plane passed through the coupler head and knuckle at the center line. The contour line would outline the shape of the knuckle, the inside face of the head, and the guard arm.

Coupler Guard Arm. That portion of the coupler head opposite the knuckle. The guard arm guides a mating coupler into position during a coupling operation and forms one side of the pocket into which the opposing coupler knuckle fits while two cars are coupled.

Coupler Head. That portion of the coupler that houses the locking mechanism. A pivot mount for the coupler knuckle is on one side of the head and the guard arm is on the opposite side.

Coupler Height. The vertical distance above the rail to the center of the coupler knuckle measured with the coupler properly installed, and the car on level, tangent track. Standard nominal coupler height for new cars (empty car) is 34-1/2".

Coupler Horn. The projecting lug cast on top of the coupler head which bears on the striker plate when the draft gear is fully compressed.

Coupler Knuckle. See Knuckle.

Coupler Lock. One of the internal components of a coupler. The lock drops into position by gravity when the knuckle closes and prevents reopening of the knuckle until the uncoupling mechanism is activated.

Coupler Lock Lifter. That part of the mechanism inside the coupler head which is activated by the uncoupling rod and lifts the lock so that the knuckle can open. Sometimes called the "lock lift."

Coupler Lock Set. A device, by which the knuckle lock when lifted is held in a raised position until the knuckle is opened at which time it allows the lock to drop back into position for automatic coupling when the cars are brought together.

Coupler Release Rigging. See Uncoupling Lever.

Coupler Shank. That part of a coupler behind the head and containing either a slot or a pinhole at the rear portion for connection to the yoke and draft system.

Coupler Yoke. A cast steel component of the draft system that functions as the connecting link between the coupler and the draft gear.

Couplet (of Springs). Two elliptic springs, placed side by side, to act as one spring.

Covered Gondola. A gondola car which has been equipped with some form of removable cover which can be placed over the lading to protect it from weather exposure in transit.

Covered Hopper Car. A hopper car with a permanent roof, roof hatches and bottom openings for unloading. Used for carrying cement, grain or other bulk commodities.

Cover Glass. A transparent glass or similar product used in an optical system to protect one or more of its components from foreign material or mechanical injury and to pass light rays without intended deviation or change of color.

Cover Plate. In steel construction, a general term referring to any flat plate connected to two other structural numbers generally at a 90 degree angle forming a "cover" over the two top members. In car construction, many underframe members are box sections with top and bottom cover plates.

Crabs or Tongs (Pile Driver and Wreck Crane). A pair of loose bent steel bars fastened at the top with a ring and intended to firmly clamp to the underside of the rail head when an upward pull is applied to the ring. They are used to anchor a pile driver car, steam shovel or wreck crane to the rails and prevent them from overturning when a heavy load is being lifted. A jack screw is used in connection with tongs to raise the body of the car and keep the tongs under strain. Also called "rail clips" or "rail clamps."

Cradle. A hinged or pivoted inclined track structure, generally on a river bank, having a horizontal deck with track thereon for transfer of railroad cars to and from boats at different elevations of water level.

Crank. That part of the crankshaft to which the connecting rod is attached.

Crankcase. The lower part of the engine structure surrounding the working parts.

Crankcase Explosion. An explosion caused by the ignition of an explosive mixture of fuel vapor and air in the crankcase of a diesel engine. The explosive mixture may result from incomplete atomization and partial combustion of the fuel injected into the combustion chamber. A spark from an overheated bearing or from interference between metal parts may cause the ignition.

Crankpin. That part of the crank to which the connecting rod is connected in an internal combustion engine.

Crank Pin. The pin used to secure a crank to a crank stand and forming a pivot.

Crank Shaft. The main rotating member of an internal combustion engine. It is made in a series of steps or cranks to which the connecting rods are attached and is carried in a number of bearings placed in the bedplate.

Crank Shaft Bearing. A bearing placed in the locomotive engine frame or bedplate that carries the crank shaft in its proper location.

Creosote. A tar distillate produced by high-temperature carbonization of bituminous coal and used in wood treatment.

Crib. The lateral space between two railroad ties. A retaining structure.

Cribbing Machine. Removes rock between ties where the rail lays.

Critical Speed (of a Car). That speed at which the frequency of lateral rocking of a freight car on its center plate is reinforced by rail joints in the track, thus increasing the magnitude of the rocking and sometimes causing a derailment.

Critical Temperatures (Steelmaking). Temperatures reached in the heating or cooling process which cause marked internal crystalline or molecular transformations to occur in iron or steel, resulting in alterations in the physical properties of the material.

Crop End. A section cut from the end of a bloom or during the manufacture of rail.

Cropping. Removal of metal from the end of an ingot bloom or rail during its manufacture. Also, cutting of the ends of used rails which are battered or damaged.

Crossarm. An arm, usually fastened at right angles to a pole, designed to carry the pins and insulators to which wires may be attached.

Cross Bar. A bar with locking devices at each end that fit and lock to belt rails in DF boxcars to provide longitudinal restraint for lading. Cross bars are sometimes called "cross members."

Crossbearer (Car Construction). A transverse member of the underframe, serving to connect the side sills to the center sill. Crossbearers generally extend completely across the car through a filler in the center sill, while cross ties are lighter members connecting the center and side sills together.

Crosshead (Air Brake Cylinder). A forked casting or forging attached to the end of the cylinder piston rod to which the brake levers are connected.

Crossing End Frogs. The two frogs located at the opposite ends of the long diagonal of a crossing.

Crossing Frogs. The two frogs located at the opposite ends of the short diagonal of a crossing.

Crossing Knuckle Rail. Derives its name from being a bent rail, or equivalent structure, which forms the blunt point against which the movable center points, of a movable point crossing or slip switch, rest when set for traffic.

Crossing Plates. Plates that are interposed between a crossing and the ties or other timbers for the purpose of protecting the ties and to better support the crossing by distributing the loads over larger areas.

Crossing Protection. Signs, signals, aspects, and other objects governing movement of trains, track equipment, and highway vehicles over railroad crossings or grade crossings.

Cross Level. The distance one rail is above or below another. This should not be confused with superelevation on curves.

Crossover. Two turnouts in which the track between the frogs is arranged to form a continuous passage between two nearby and generally parallel tracks.

Crossover Platform. A drop step located on the engine front and rear permitting movement of personnel between units.

Cross Section. A vertical section of any object, depicting the object as it would be seen if projected on a vertical plane in which it passes through.

Cross Tie. The transverse member of the track structure to which the rails are spiked or otherwise fastened to provide proper gage and to cushion, distribute, and transmit the stresses of traffic through the ballast to the roadbed.

Crown. That portion of a roller bearing adapter casting that bears on the pedestal roof of a truck side frame.

C.T.C. The abbreviation for centralized traffic control.

Cubic Capacity. The number of cubic feet of lading that can be loaded into a car.

Cupola. A small cabin on the roof of a caboose to afford a means of lookout for the train crew.

Curb. As used in tunnel construction, a broad flat ring made of wood, iron or masonry placed under the bottom of a shaft to prevent unequal settlement, or built into the walls at intervals for the same purpose.

Current of Traffic. The movement of trains on a main track, in one direction, specified by the rules.

Curve (of a Railroad Line). In the United States, it is customary to express track curvature in degrees noted by the deflection from the tangent measured at stations 100 feet apart. In other words, the number of degrees of central angle subtended by a chord of 100 feet represents the "degree curve." One degree of curvature is equal to a radius of 5,750 feet.

Cushioned Underframe. A term generally used to describe a freight car designed with a center sill arranged so that a hydraulically cushioned inner sill, free to slide with respect to a rigid outer sill, absorbs a major portion of the end impact loads experienced in switching. Not to be confused with end-of-car cushioning devices, which are independent units installed in the draft gear pockets behind each coupler.

Cushioning. A term referring to the energy-absorbing capabilities of a car underframe or draft system. Although standard draft gears do have energy-absorbing capabilities, the term "cushioning" or "hydraulic cushioning" is generally understood to mean systems with a minimum travel of ten inches.

Cut. A passage cut for the roadway through an obstacle of rock or dirt.

Cut (of Cars). A group of cars coupled together that are to be moved as a unit (generally, either to be added or dropped from a train).

Cut-out. An electrical device to interrupt the flow of current through any particular apparatus or instrument, either automatically or by hand.

Cutout Cock. A valve in the branch pipe of an air brake system that can be closed to nullify the brake on an individual car without affecting the brakes on adjacent cars. On modern freight cars, the cutout cock is combined with a dirt collector, or strainer, to keep foreign matter from entering the control valve, and the assembly is known as a "combination dirt collector and cutout cock." In general terms, a cutout cock is any valve inserted in a piping system that allows flow to be shut off to a particular branch of that system.

Cut-Section. A location other than a signal location where two adjoining track circuits end within a block. (I.C.C.)

Cutting Torch. A tool used in oxygen cutting operations for controlling and directing the gases used for preheating, and the oxygen used for cutting the metal.

Cycle. In general terms, a complete series of operations which occur in a repetitious manner. A complete cycle has occured when the last operation has been completed and the first operation is about to begin again.

Cylinder. Any enclosed chamber, generally of circular cross-section, fitted with a piston for transforming the energy of a compressed fluid into linear motion for some useful purpose. See Brake Cylinder.

Cylinder Head. The closure over the end of a cylinder, generally secured with bolts or studs. The pressure head is on the end of the cylinder under pressure, while the non-pressure head closes the end where no pressure exists.

Cylinder Lever. The brake lever in the body or foundation rigging that transmits the braking force from the brake cylinder to the floating lever.

Cylinder Lever Guide. A U-shaped bar or bracket fastened to the car underframe that supports and guides the cylinder lever during operation of the air brakes.

Cylinder Liner (Engine). A tube placed in the cylinder block that takes the wear of the piston and forms the cylinder itself.

Cylinder Support. A bracket attached to the car underframe to which the brake cylinder is attached.

D

Damage Claim (Freight). A demand upon the carrier for reimbursement for physical injury to shipment or because shipment was not delivered within a reasonable time.

Damages. Compensation, usually in money, for injury to goods, person or property.

Dampener. Any material or device used to reduce vibration.

Dating Nail. A nail the head of which has a raised or depressed number or symbol and which is driven into a longitudinal surface of a pile, pole, tie, or timber to identify the year in which the material was treated.

Dead Cylinder Lever. That part of the foundation brake gear connected to the live cylinder lever by a tie rod and to the live truck lever by the top rod.

Dead Head. An operating term used to describe off-duty travel of a train crew member from some point back to his or her home terminal. Sometimes the term is used to identify any railroad employee traveling on a pass.

Dead Head Traffic. Freight or passengers, usually company materials and employees traveling on free passes, transported without assessment of tariff rates.

Dead Lever. A truck brake lever, the upper end of which is attached to the dead lever guide. Depending on the type of truck brake arrangement, the lower end of the dead lever is either connected to the truck bottom rod (rod under arrangement) or to the brake beam strut (rod through arrangement) with the center hole being pinned to the remaining member.

Dead Lever Guide. A steel strap in the form of an elongated "U" attached to either the truck bolster or a point on the car underframe, the function of which is to provide the fulcrum point for the truck dead lever. Dead lever guides on older cars have a series of holes for the purpose of adjusting truck brake rigging to compensate for wheel and brake shoe wear. Single hole dead lever guides are generally used on cars equipped with automatic slack adjusters. Also called "brake lever stop."

Deadlight. In passenger car construction the panel between two adjacent windows.

Dead Load. In car design calculations, the weight of the car body with all attachments and appurtenances that will be supported by the trucks. See Live Load.

Deadman. A means for providing anchorage for a guy or cable, consisting of a timber or piece of structural steel buried in the ground, to which is fastened (generally around the middle) the end of the guy line or cable.

Deadman Control. A pedal or handle, or both, one of which must be kept in a depressed position while a locomotive is operating; usually the brake-valve handle and a pedal which the engineman can conveniently keep depressed at his seat. When pressure is released from both at the same time they function to cut off the power and apply the brakes.

Dead Section. A section of track either within a track circuit or between two track circuits, the rails of which are not part of a track circuit. (I.C.C.)

Decal. Any lettering or design work printed on a transparent film with a backing which is removed when subjected to water soaking.

Decelostat Equipment. A combination of devices used to measure the rate of retardation and to cause a rapid reduction of brake-cylinder pressure when a wheel slip is starting.

Deck Bridge. A bridge in which the supporting structure is entirely beneath the track.

Deck Span Bridge. A bridge in which the track is carried on top of the stringers (girders) or trusses.

Declared (Valuation) Rate. A transportation charge (rate) based upon a declared valuation.

Defect Card. A card issued by a railroad acknowledging responsibility for physical damage done to a non-owned railroad car and granting authority to bill the issuing carrier for the cost of repairs in accordance with the code of Interchange Rules published by the Association of American Railroads.

Defect Card Holder. A metal or plastic receptacle positioned on the side of a car suitable for the containment and protection of defect cards.

Deferred Maintenance. The accrued expenses chargeable to current operations for the estimated cost of repairs which cannot be made during the year due to priorities for materials and supplies or shortage of labor.

Density. Weight per unit of volume, generally expressed as pounds per cubic foot or pounds per gallon in the English system; or kilograms per cubic meter, or kilograms per liter, in the Metric system.

Density of Traffic. The tonnage or volume of traffic over any section or division of a railroad measured in terms of carloads or ton-miles.

Departure Track. One of the tracks in a departure yard on which outgoing cars are placed.

Departure Yard. A rail yard where trains are assembled and made ready for departure.

Depreciation. The decrease in value of a piece of equipment over time.

Depressed Center Flatcar. A flatcar having that portion of the deck between the trucks lower or closer to the rail to accomodate loads with excessive vertical dimensions.

Depth (of Ballast). The depth measurement from the bottom of the tie to the top of the subgrade.

Derail. A safety device, attached to one rail of a siding or storage track, that will cause a car to be derailed in the event it rolls free towards a main track where it could cause a major accident.

Derailment. Anytime the wheels of a car or engine come off the head of the rail.

Detail Fracture. A progressive fracture starting at or near the surface of the rail head. Such fractures are entirely different from transverse fissures, compound fissures or other defects which have internal origins.

Detention. The act of holding a car longer than the specified free time for loading and unloading. See Demurrage.

DF. A term used to describe an interior lading restraint system for boxcars, using transverse bars (cross bars) engaging special belt rails mounted to the car sides. The initials DF stand for "damage free." See Cross Bar.

Diaphragm. A thin elastomeric component used in some valve portions of railway air brake equipment to sense pressure differentials and initiate desired movement of other internal valve components. In passenger car contruction, a diaphragm is a rubber or canvas shield used to exclude dust and water from the passageway between two cars.

Diesel-Electric Locomotive. A locomotive in which power developed by one or more diesel engines is converted to electrical energy and delivered to the traction motors for propulsion.

Diesel Engine. An internal combustion engine invented by Rudolf Diesel differing from other internal combustion engines because its compression is high enough to cause combustion without the necessity of introducing a spark for ignition.

Diesel-Hydraulic Locomotive. A locomotive in which power developed by one or more diesel engines is delivered through a hydraulic transmission to the driving axles by means of shafts and gears.

Differential Rate. A rate established via a route from one point to another by deducting a fixed amount from, or adding a fixed amount to the rate via another route between the same points.

Dining Car. A passenger train car equipped with facilities for serving meals.

Diode. The simplest of the various forms of semi-conductors that allows electric current to flow in one direction only.

Direct Current. An electric current that flows in one direction only.

Dirt Collector. A device installed in the air brake system of a freight car used to prevent foreign matter from entering the control valve. See Cutout Cock.

Disc Brake. A retardation system used on some rail vehicles, primarily passenger equipment, which utilizes flat steel discs as the braking surface instead of the wheel tread as on conventional brakes.

Discharge Pipe (Air Compressor). A pipe by which the compressed air is conveyed from the air compressor to the main air reservoir.

Discrimination. As defined by the Interstate Commerce Act, discrimination exists when certain commodities, industries or communities are granted or enjoy privileges which are at the same time not allowed or available to others entitled to them.

Disc Signal. A signal in which a colored disc is displayed behind a glass front in a closed case.

Dispatcher. The individual who plans and controls the movement of trains.

Distant Signal. A fixed signal used to govern the approach to an interlocking signal.

District. On some railroads, the part of the railroad under the jurisdiction of a District Superintendent.

Diversion. Interchangeable with "Reconsignment;" refers to the practice of changing the billing or destination of a shipment either before or after it reaches the originally billed destination.

Division. On some railroads, the part of a railroad generally under the control of a Division Superintendent.

Division of Revenue. The share of revenue enjoyed by one carrier in an interline movement.

Dog. A term sometimes used when referring to the hand brake pawl. A dog is more properly an eccentrically pivoted disc, the function of which is to hold a pawl in place against a ratchet wheel.

Dog Chart. A diagrammatic representation of the mechanical locking for an interlocking machine, used as a working plan in making-up, assembling and fitting.

Dolly. A small square or rectangular-shaped material handling device consisting of a frame on wheels or casters.

Dome. A closed vertical cylinder attached to the top of a tank car which provides for expansion of the contents.

Dome Car. A passenger car constructed with a raised area in the center of the car with a transparent roof for passenger observation.

Dome Cover. The closure for the top of a tank car dome.

Door. A general term used to designate either an opening in a freight car for loading and/or unloading, or the component that forms the closure for that opening.

Door Guide. A bracket attached to sliding side doors on boxcars, serving to guide the door while it is being opened and closed and to keep it in proper vertical alignment.

Door Hanger. A device by which a sliding door is suspended at the top. Most modern freight car door hangers are fitted with rollers which run on a door track.

Door Hasp. On freight cars with sliding side doors, a heavy metal strap with a slot that fits over a staple on the door post to secure the door in the closed position. After placing the hasp over the staple, a wedge-staple pin is driven through the staple to secure the hasp and a car seal is passed through a small hole in the bottom of the pin.

Door Lifting Lever. A device that raises a boxcar door off the door track and throws the weight upon the rollers thus allowing the door to be moved easily.

Door Roller. A solid steel roller secured in an assembly at the top and/or bottom of sliding side doors which carries the weight of the door and rolls on the door track to facilitate opening and closing.

Door Sill. A cross piece attached to the floor at the door opening.

Door Starter. Any one of several devices with high mechanical advantage used to facilitate initial movement of a sliding side door from its closed position.

Door Stop. A steel casting welded or bolted to the side of a car that serves to limit the rearward travel of the door.

Door Track. A steel angle or channel fastened to the car side at the top and/or bottom of the door opening to secure and support the door and provide the running surface for the door rollers.

DOT. The Department of Transportation. An agency of the U.S. government having jurisdiction over matters pertaining to all modes of transportation. The Federal Railroad Administration is the branch of the DOT that promulgates safety standards for rail equipment used in interchange.

Double Crossover. Two crossovers which intersect and form a continuous passage between the connected tracks.

Double Deck. A second floor in a stock car halfway between the ordinary floor and the roof to increase the carrying capacity of the car for small livestock such as pigs and sheep.

Double Door Car. Boxcars having two side doors on each side of car. May be plug, sliding or combination of both.

Double-Slip Switch. A combination of a crossing and two connecting tracks, located within the limits of the crossing, each being made up of a right-hand switch from the one track and a left-hand switch from the other track, which unite to form the respective connecting tracks without additional frogs.

Double Transom Truck. A four-wheel passenger truck with two bolsters designed to give the same riding qualities as the six-wheel truck.

Dowel. A peg or pin of metal or wood which extends into, but through, two members of the structure to connect them.

Dowel Pin. A pin used to accurately maintain the proper alignment between two parts.

Draft. A term used to describe forces resulting in tension in the coupler shank. The term "draft" means the opposite of the term "buff."

Draft Gear. A term used to describe the energy-absorbing component of the draft system. The draft gear is installed in a yoke which is connected to the coupler shank and is fitted with follower blocks which contact the draft lugs on the car center sill. So-called "standard" draft gear use rubber and/or friction components to provide energy absorption, while "hydraulic" draft gear use a closed hydraulic system consisting of small ports and a piston to achieve a greater energy-absorbing capability. Hydraulic draft gear assemblies are generally called "cushioning units." See Cushioning.

Draft Gear Carrier. A steel plate extending underneath and fastened to the draft sill flanges to support the draft gear or cushion unit.

Draft Gear Cheek Castings. Castings welded to the draft sills which serve as stops for the draft gear followers through which the pulling and buffing forces are transmitted to the center sills. These may be four separate castings but generally each pair (front and rear) is cast together as a center-sill filler.

Draft Gear Pocket. The space in the draft sill that contains the energy-absorbing components of the draft system. The draft gear pocket is formed by the draft sill top cover plate, the draft sill webs, the front and read draft lugs, and the draft gear carrier plate.

Draft Key. A heavy steel bar used to connect the coupler shank to the yoke.

Draft Key Retainer. A pin inserted at one end of the draft key to prevent it from backing out through the slot in the center sills.

Draft Lug. One of a set of stops riveted, bolted or welded to the draft sills and transmitting to them the stresses received from the draft gear.

Draft Sill. That portion of the car center sill outboard of the body bolster containing the various components of the draft system.

Draft System. The term used to describe the arrangement on a car for transmitting coupler forces to the center sill. On standard draft gear cars, the draft system includes the coupler, yoke, draft gear, follower, draft key, draft lugs and draft sill. On cushioned cars, either hydraulic end-of-car cushion units and their attachments replace the draft gear and yoke at each end; or a hydraulically controlled sliding center sill is installed as an integral part of the car underframe.

Drag. A common expression to describe the movement of a heavy train, such as a "coal drag" or an "ore drag."

Drain Valve. In passenger car steam heat systems, a valve used for draining off the water condensed in the steam pipes where an automatic trap is not used.

Drawbar. A term formerly used synonymously with coupler. It has been used indiscriminately to designate both the old link and pin drawbar and the modern automatic car coupler.

Drawbar Pull. A tensile coupler force. Locomotive pulling power is sometimes expressed in terms of "pounds of drawbar pull."

Drawbridge. Another term to describe a movable bridge.

Draw Head. The head of an automatic coupler.

Drift Bolt. A piece of steel which may be round or square, with or without head or point and of specified length, driven as a spike.

Drift Pin. A special railroad tool of round steel tapered for insertion to align holes by striking the large end.

Drilling. The switching or handling of cars in freight yards.

Drill Track. A track connecting with the ladder track, over which locomotives and cars move back and forth in switching.

Driving Wheel. Any of the powered wheels under a locomotive.

Drop Bottom Car. A gondola car with a level floor or bottom equipped with a number of drop doors for discharging the load.

Drop Door. A door at the bottom of a hopper or gondola car for unloading it quickly by allowing the load to fall through the opening.

Drop End Gondola Car. A gondola car with ends which can be dropped when the car is used for shipping long material which extends over more than one car.

Drop Forging. One made by the use of dies under a drop hammer.

Drop Shaft Brake. A horizontal wheel hand brake for flatcars with an arrangement for lowering the handwheel close to the floor to accommodate lading.

Drop Table. Shop equipment used to lower car or locomotive trucks from under the superstructure.

Drop Test. The ductility and impact resistance of finished metal shapes is determined by the drop test which uses a fixed weight falling from a predetermined height and delivering a blow or shock to the metal shape, which rests on supports attached to an anvil. A similar test (called a "drop hammer" test) conducted under highly controlled and instrumented conditions is used to certify AAR approved draft gears.

Drum (Hoisting Gear). The main cylinder upon which the hoisting rope winds and unwinds.

Drum Shaft (of a Derrick or Crane). The shaft on which the winding drum is carried.

Dry Cell. A primary cell using zinc as the positive electrode, carbon as the negative electrode and ammonium chloride for the electrolyte.

Dual Control. A term applied to signal appliances provided with two authorized methods of operation.

Dual Control Switch. A power-operated switch which is also equipped for hand operation.

Ductility. A physical property of a material relating to its ability to be stretched, drawn or hammered to permit permanent distortion without rupture. Ductility, or "workability" usually varies inversely with tensile strength.

Dummy Hose Coupling (Air Brake). A casting, the same shape as a hose coupling, into which the coupling may be hooked. It is used to prevent dirt and debris from getting into the brake pipe, as well as preventing the coupling hose from hanging down when not in use and being damaged. Dummy couplings are also used to seal off the brake hose during tests of the air brake equipment on cars.

Dummy Mast. A short upright displaying a blue reflector, placed on top of a bracket post or bracketed to the side of a signal mast, to show that there is a track between the bracket post or signal mast, and the track for which the signal is provided.

Dump Car. A car from which the load is discharged either through doors or by tipping the car body.

Dunnage. Waste material such as wooden blocks or steel pads used to support and secure lading in or on a freight car.

Dust Collector. A device for preventing dust or pipe scale from passing to an air brake valve mechanism. It usually operates on a centrifugal system of separating the foreign particles from the air.

Dust Guard. A thin piece of material inserted in the dust guard chamber at the back of a journal box and fitting closely around the dust guard bearing of the axle. It is used to exclude dirt and prevent the escape of oil.

Dwarf Signal. A low home signal. (Standard Code)

Dynamic Brake Regulator. A device which prevents braking grid amperage from exceeding a predetermined value.

Dynamic Braking. A term used to describe a method of train braking whereby the kinetic energy of a moving train is used to generate electric current at the locomotive traction motors, which is then dissipated through banks of resistor grids in the locomotive car body.

Dynamic Braking Resistors. Grid resistors which are mounted just under the roof of the locomotive. The power from the traction motors, operating as generators during dynamic braking, is dissipated through the resistors.

Dynamite. A slang term used to describe the initiation of an emergency air brake application on a train.

Dynamiter. A slang term for a car with a defective control valve which will create an emergency brake application and serially propagate the emergency application throughout the train even though such action was not desired by the crew. Common causes are stuck valves in the car's control valve, or the opening of these valves due to the vibration and/or slack action of the car. Also called "kicker."

Dynamometer. A device for determining the power of an engine.

Dynamometer Car. A car equipped with apparatus for measuring and recording drawbar pull, horsepower, brake pipe pressure, and other data connected with locomotive performance and train haul conditions.

E

"E" Coupler. A standard A.A.R. automatic coupler. Type "E" couplers are cast in several grades of steel, and have several shank configurations to meet varying service requirements.

Easement. A curve, the degree of which varies in a predetermined manner to give a gradual transition between curves.

Easer Rail. A rail placed with its head along the outside and close up to the head of the running rail and sloped at the ends to provide a bearing for the overhanging portion of hollowed-out treads of worn wheels.

Eave. The edge of the roof projection over the sides of a car.

Eddy Current. A local current in an iron core caused by the electromotive force generated by moving the core in a magnetic field.

Eddy Current Clutch. A magnetic clutch on some Alco locomotives which connects the radiator fan with an engine-driven shaft without a mechanical connection.

Effective Date. The date a standard, specification, design, product or device, must be placed in effect for equipment interchange service. (A.A.R.)

Efficiency. A general term that defines the ratio of output to input in any system.

Electrically Locked Switch. A hand-operated switch equipped with an electrically controlled device which restricts the movement of the switch.

Electric Circuit. See Circuit, Electric.

Electric Current. The quantity of electrical energy flowing in a circuit.

Electric Flash Butt Weld. A weld made by electrically heating two abutting rail ends. When the steel reaches the proper temperature, the rail ends are compressed together, eliminating the need for joint bars.

Electric Furnace. A steelmaking furnace in which the source of heat is low voltage high current electricity..

Electric Generator. A rotating device used to produce electricity. A generator is usually assumed to produce direct current while alternating current is produced with an alternator.

Electric Heater. A heater powered by electricity passing through resistance coils with appropriate control and regulating devices.

Electricity. An imponderable and invisible force producing light, heat, chemical decomposition and other physical phenomena.

Electric Locker. A locker in which the electrical control devices for lighting or air conditioning are housed.

Electric Locomotive. As distinguished from a gas-electric or diesel-electric locomotive, a self-propelled vehicle, running on rails and having one or more electric motor that drive the wheels and thereby propel the locomotive and train. The motors obtain electrical energy either from a rail laid near to, but insulated from, the track rails or from a wire suspended above the track. Contact with the wire is made by a pantograph or trolley wheel on the end of a pole mounted on top of the locomotive.

Electric Motor. A rotating machine powered by electricity.

Electric Motor Car. A vehicle for operation on track rails, used for the transport of passengers or materials, the propulsion of which is effected by electric motors mounted on the vehicle.

Electric Trainline. A continuous electric conductor extended between cars by means of jumper cables or couplers so that power or control signals can be transmitted to and/or from each car to permit simultaneous control of traction motors and other vehicle carried equipment. An electric trainline may include circuits for auxiliary electric brakes, communication, engine controls and other devices.

Electric Valve. A valve, the operation of which is controlled by electricity.

Electrification. A term used to describe the installation of overhead wire or third rail power distribution facilities to enable operation of trains hauled by electric locomotives.

Electrified Territory. That portion of a railroad equipped with all the facilities necessary for operation of trains hauled by electric locomotives or electric MU cars.

Electromagnet. A device comprising one or more coils of insulated wire wound around an iron or steel core, and depending for its magnetic action upon the passage of an electric current through the wire.

Electromotive Force. The electrical force which maintains a current of electricity. The potential or voltage developed by a battery or generator.

Electronic Alertness Control (Alerter). A type of safety control system involving a low-powered radio frequency circuit that senses the movements of an engineman. The locomotive engineer's seat is equipped with a built-in antenna. As the locomotive engineer goes about his normal activity, such as adjusting the throttle position or applying the brakes, sanding, blowing the horn, etc., these motions produce a detectable change in the energy output of the seat antenna. Any such changes will reset the control and start a timing circuit.

Electronics. That branch of science and technology which relates to the conduction of electricity through gases or in a vacuum. (I.E.E.E.)

Electro-Pneumatic Brake. A braking system used on high-speed electric passenger trains. Brakes are applied and released on each car through the action of electro-pneumatic valves energized by current taken from contacts on the motorman's brake valve and continuous train wires. Brakes can be applied instantaneously and simultaneously with this device, eliminating undesirable slack action and providing more positive control of train speed.

Elevation. In general, the vertical distance that some location is above some reference location, usually sea level. In railroad trackwork, the vertical distance that the outer rail is above the inner rail on a curve is called "the elevation (or superelevation) of the curve."

Elliptic Spring. A spring whose shape resembles an ellipse. Made of two sets of parallel steel plates called "leaves," of constantly decreasing length. Such springs were once widely used for bolster springs for passenger cars.

Elongation. In physical testing, the percent of change from the original gage length of a test specimen when tested to rupture in tension.

Embankment (or Fill). A bank of earth, rock or other material constructed above the natural ground surface.

Embargo. A method of controlling traffic movements when accumulations, threatened congestions, or other interferences with normal operations of a temporary nature, compel restrictions against acceptance or movement of traffic.

Emergency Application (Air Brake). The type of brake application made when a train must be stopped in the minimum distance possible for the equipment. It may be made from the Conductor's Valve or from the Engineer's Brake Valve on the locomotive or power car. An emergency application may also occur when a brake pipe is broken or when air hoses between cars are disconnected when angle cocks are open. An emergency application is brought about by the very rapid exhausting of air pressure from the brake pipe, and results in a correspondingly rapid build-up of brake cylinder pressure.

Emergency Coupler. A short shank coupler which can be chained in place if the standard coupler is pulled out or broken.

Emergency Knuckle. A coupler knuckle which is designed for use in case of damage to the knuckle of an automatic coupler.

Emergency Portion (Air Brake). One of three parts of the air brake control valve. The emergency portion controls the buildup of brake cylinder pressure during emergency brake applications, and, in the ABDW control valve, contributes the improved performance (quicker response) during service applications.

Emergency Reservoir. A compressed air storage tank; part of the air brake equipment on each car. Air stored in the emergency reservoir is used to apply the brakes during an emergency application, and to assist in releasing the brakes and recharging the system during brake release operations. See Auxiliary Reservoir.

Eminent Domain. The right or soverign power to take private property for public purposes (such as to build coal slurry pipelines) with compensation.

Empty-and-Load Brakes. A brake arrangement used on some freight cars that allows for two levels of braking, depending on whether the car is empty or loaded. Empty and load brakes are required when the difference between the empty and loaded gross weights of the car is greater than can be accommodated with single capacity brake equipment within the braking limits established by the Association of American Railroads.

Empty Car-Miles. Mileage of freight cars without load, as opposed to "loaded car-miles."

End Chipping. Metal that has been loosened on the top or gage side of the end of a rail.

End Door. A door arrangement in the end of a boxcar generally used for loading long commodities that cannot be loaded easily through side doors.

End Frame. The frame which forms the end of a car body. It includes the posts, braces, belt rail and end plate.

End Hardening. A process whereby head treatment is applied to the top portion of the heads of rails at the ends to minimize rail batter.

End Loading. See Circus Loading.

End-of-Car Cushioning Device. A unit installed at the ends of a car that develops energy-absorbing capacity through a hydraulic piston arrangement supplemented by springs to assure positive repositioning of the unit. These devices replace the standard draft gear, and provide up to 15 inches of travel.

End Overflow. A projection of metal into the rail joint gap at the top or side of the head of a rail.

End Plate. A member across the end and connecting the tops of the end posts of a car body and fastened at the ends to the two side plates. It is usually made of the proper form to serve as an end carline.

End Play (Axle). The movement or space left for movement between journals. In reference to truck bolster, it is usually called "lateral motion."

End Post. The vertical members in the end body framing between the corner posts. With reference to hopper cars, a vertical support for the overhang of the hopper floor, resting on the end sill.

End Sheet. A plate used in closing the end of a steel car.

End Sill. The transverse member of the underframe of a car extending across the ends of all the longitudinal sills. In steel underframe cars, a rolled or cast section or a pressed plate.

End Sill Brackets. Angle plates used to connect the longitudinal sills and the end sill. In bridge building such plates are termed brackets. When of triangular section they are termed "gussets."

End Sill Diagonal Brace. A horizontal brace extending from the end sill diagonally back to or beyond the bolster.

End Sill Plate. A plate extending the full length and width of a built-up end sill, and attached to the other members.

End Slope. The sloping floor from the end of a hopper car to the hopper door. See Slope Sheet.

Endurance Limit. The highest unit stress, the repeated application of which can be indefinitely endured without failure.

Engine. A mechanism for converting the energy in steam, air or other gas under pressure into mechanical energy in the form of motion. Usually restricted to reciprocating engines having a cylinder, reciprocating piston and means for causing the gas under pressure to expand alternately on one or both sides of the piston and move it back and forth in the cylinder. The term also includes the means of transforming the reciprocating motion of the piston into rotary motion, usually consisting of a connecting rod and crank. Frequently used as meaning the entire locomotive. See Internal Combustion Engine.

Engine Base. In a locomotive, the structure on which the engine frame is supported and which is bolted to the locomotive frame.

Engine Burn Fracture. A rail failure which originates in spots where driving wheels have slipped on top of the rail head. In developing downward, they frequently resemble the compound or even transverse fissure, with which they should not be confused or classified.

Engineer. See Engineman.

Engineering Report. A report compiled by the Interstate Commerce Commission in connection with the federal valuation, showing the physical property of a railway as inventoried (except "land"), classified according to ownership and use by units, unit prices and totals, purporting to give the estimated cost of reproduction new and reproduction less depreciation of a railway at a given date of valuation.

Engine Frame. In an internal combustion engine, the structural frame of the engine in which are secured the cylinder liners and water jackets. Sometimes referred to as "crankcase" or "cylinder block."

Enginehouse. Facilities provided for maintaining locomotives and making light repairs.

Engineman. The driver or operator of a locomotive or locomotive consist.

English Bond. The manner of laying bricks in a structure in which each alternate course is composed entirely of headers or of stretches.

Envelope Air Distribution. A form of air distribution for refrigerator cars in which all of the cooled or heated air is passed in ducts and flues between the lading space and the insulated outer structure.

Environmental Impact Statement. A statement based on studies of economics, ecology, etc. which railroads are required to file with the Interstate Commerce Commission concerning the effect on the environment which would result from the transfer of rail freight traffic to other modes before a petition for abandonment of a railroad branch line may be considered by the I.C.C.

Epoxy Resins. Thermosetting resins made by polymerization of an epoxide and used chiefly in coatings and adhesives. In railroad service they are used as electrical insulation.

Equalizer. In six-wheel and some four-wheel truck arrangements, a system of bars, rods, levers and springs that serves to equalize the loads on the axles and provide improved riding qualities for the truck.

Equalizer Spring. A spring which rests on an equalizing bar and carries part of the weight of a car. Single or double coil spiral or helical springs are generally used for this purpose.

Equalizing Brake Lever. A floating brake lever used to equalize forces in the brake rigging.

Equalizing Lever Set. An arrangement of cylinder levers and connections for double-truck cars, so designed to ensure proper equalization of braking force on both trucks with either the hand or air brake.

Equilibrium Speed. The speed of a train on a curve at which the axle loads are evenly divided between both rails.

Equipment. In general, the rolling stock of a railroad including both locomotives and cars.

Escutcheon. A plate or guard for the keyhole of a lock.

Estimated Tare. An estimated light weight (empty weight) of a car or container.

Evaporation. The conversion of a liquid to the gaseous state.

Ex. or X (Out Of). Used in connection with rolling stock, it means that contents of car designated "Ex (or X)" car had previously been transferred from that car to the one now holding the goods.

Examiner (I.C.C.). A representative of the Interstate Commerce

Commission with power to administer oaths, examine witnesses and take testimony, and assigned to conduct hearings in various parts of the country.

Exciter. An auxiliary generator which supplies power for the field excitation of another electrical machine. (I.E.E.E.)

Exchange Bill of Lading. A bill of lading issued in exchange for another, or receipt for a shipment.

Exhaust. The products of combustion from an engine cylinder. Also, the air discharge from the brake pipe or brake cylinder during operation of the brake equipment.

Exhaust Manifold. A conduit connecting each cylinder of the engine to a common outlet to carry the burned gases to the exhaust pipe.

Exhaust Stack. The ducts placed on top of the hood or cab to convey the exhaust gases away from the locomotive.

Exhaust Valve. Any valve that controls the flow of exhaust air or products of combustion.

Expansion Cycle (Internal Combustion Engines). The portion of the power stroke during which the combustion gases exert pressure on the moving piston and expand while the pressure falls.

Expansion Shim. Spacer inserted between ends of abutting rails while track is being laid to provide allowance for expansion of steel when temperature changes.

Ex Parte (Latin). From only one side or party.

Explosives & Dangerous Articles. Those commodities singled out as easily combustible or capable of combusting spontaneously, the transport of which, when permitted, may be made only under certain prescribed conditions. See Hazardous Material.

Express Car. A specially constructed car, operated in passenger trains and used for transportation of express shipments; sometimes combined with facilities for handling baggage or mail.

Express Train. A passenger train operating on fast schedule and not stopping at all stations on its route; also a train consisting of "Express Freight."

Extended Range Dynamic Brake. A dynamic brake control for low train speed operation, which increases the braking effort in speed ranges down to about 6 mph. High braking grid amperage is obtained by the controls which automatically short out the braking grid resistance in small increments as train speed reduces below about 23 mph. This feature may also be referred to as "Variable Speed Braking."

Extension Handles. Lifting handles applied to maintenance-of-way motor cars or other light work equipment, so designed that they pull out from the body of the car or equipment. Facilitates the removal of equipment from track by increasing the leverage obtained.

Exterior Heater Pipes. A general term used to identify all heating systems which consist of outside mounted pipes or coils.

Extraordinary Value. A term in freight classification denoting a degree of value which prohibits the movement of the goods so classed by regular freight, or if so, only under certain specified conditions.

Extra Train. A train not represented on the timetable.

F

Fabrication (Tariff Provision). A privilege afforded shippers whereby shipments of iron and steel may be stopped enroute to allow for certain assembly operations related to the end use of the material, later to be forwarded to destination, the through rate from point of origin to destination applicable.

Fabrication (Steel Construction). The assembly of parts or components by bolting, welding or other mechanical means.

Face. When used with reference to steel wheels, the face of the rim is the outside surface of the rim of the wheel.

Facing Movement. The movement of a train over the points of a switch which face in a direction opposite to that in which the train is moving. (I.C.C.)

Facing Point Switch. A track switch, the points of which face traffic approaching in the direction for which the track is signaled.

Facture. An invoice or bill of goods.

Fail Safe. A term used to designate a design principle of any system the objective of which is to eliminate the hazardous effects of a failure of the system by having the failure result in nonhazardous consequences.

False Proceed (Railway Signal Indication). A clear or green signal displayed when a more restrictive indication should be displayed because of conditions ahead. Sometimes called "False Clear."

False Restrictive Aspect. A signal aspect that conveys an indication more restrictive than intended.

FAST. An acronym for The Facility for Accelerated Service Testing located at the Transportation Test Center near Pueblo, Colorado.

Fastenings. Joint bars, bolts and spikes or other alternatives to spikes used in track construction.

Fatigue. A type of failure brought about by repeated cycles of load on a rail or other structural component.

F-Coupler. An alternate standard freight car coupler having the head portion cast in a special configuration that results in less free slack and restricted vertical movement between mating couplers. Cars equipped with F-couplers must have special flexible spring-supported coupler carriers to compensate for the loss of vertical freedom between couplers.

Federal Railroad Administration. An agency of the U.S. Department of Transportation with jurisdiction over matters of railroad safety and research.

Federal Trade Commission. A government body created for the purpose of investigating trade practices and to report on the legality of mergers, interlocked directorates and competitive activity in business.

Feeder Line. The name applied to a branch or to short line railroad, traversing territory untouched by the trunk lines and interchanging traffic at connecting points.

Feed Valve. A valve which automatically maintains a predetermined pressure of air supplied through the brake valve to the automatic brake system. It may be attached either to the brake valve or placed in the piping between the main reservoir and the brake valve.

Ferry Push Car. A very long platform car used for pushing or pulling other cars on or off a ferryboat when the latter is approached by an incline too steep for locomotives, so that the latter can push or pull the cars without running on the incline.

Fiber Optics. Light transmission through very fine flexible glass rods by internal reflection.

Field (Electricity). The magnetic flux set up by an electric current in a conductor. The magnetic flux between the poles of a motor or generator caused by the current in the field coils.

Field Coil. A coil of insulated copper wire or ribbon surrounding an iron pole of a motor field magnet. Electric current passing through these coils produces the magnetic flux in which the armature rotates, and which is called the "magnetic field."

Field Loop Control. A type of dynamic brake control which requires a special jumper cable in addition to the main jumper cable between locomotive units that are coupled together.

Field Magnet. In an electric motor or generator, the iron core and the coil surrounding it.

Field Manual. One of two manuals that together form the Association of American Railroads Code of Interchange Rules governing the condition and repair of railway equipment used in interchange service. The Field Manual contains technical information concerning mechanical condition, wear limits and repair criteria for interchange cars.

Field Side. The side of a rail away from the gage side.

Field Strength (Electrical). The density of magnetic flux between the poles of a motor.

Field Weld. A weld joining two rails together after rails are installed in track.

Fifth Wheel. The supporting plate and pivot at the forward end of a highway trailer.

Filament. A slender wire used as the incandescent conductor of an electric lamp.

Filing (of Tariffs). In its general sense this term means the placing of documents and publications where they can be located and referred to readily. As applied to regulating bodies, such as the Interstate Commerce Commission, filing means that tariffs, supplements, reissues and other schedules must be in the hands of that body at a certain time prior to effective date.

Filler Block (Trackwork). A steel block molded and designed to keep uniform the angle spread between lead and turnout rails and frogs, etc.

Filler Metal. In welding processes, metal to be added to the joint between the two members to be joined.

Fillet. A rounded corner on the inside of the angle where two surfaces join as in a casting or a machined part such as an axle journal.

Fillet Weld. A weld of approximately triangular cross section joining two surfaces at approximately right angles in either a lap, tee, or corner joint.

Final Valuation. A report of the Interstate Commerce Commission in pursuance of its work under Section 19a of the Interstate Commerce Act, showing its findings and the single sum values (final values for rate making purposes), as determined by the commission after formal proceedings, of the property of a railway company held for and used in the service of transportation.

Finance Docket. Interstate Commerce Commission's dockets on which are listed, for consideration and decision, questions relating to abandonment, extensions, consolidations and financing of common carriers.

Finger Rack. A term used to describe a special tie-down system installed on flat cars for handling long steel reinforcing bars. The car is referred to as a finger rack car and is so-named because the racks consist of a series of vertical posts, or fingers, spaced across the car deck that act as separators for the load.

Fireman (Obsolete). A person who fed fuel to the fire box on steam locomotives and also monitored the water level in the boiler.

First Class. Rail passenger travel in equipment other than coaches, such as parlor cars, sleeping cars, etc. Accommodations such as chairs, berths, bedrooms, etc. are "reserved" for travelers.

Fish-Belly Sill. A term used to describe a type of center sill construction consisting of shallow sections at each end with transitions to a deep section at the center. Fish-belly sills are often used on long cars which need heavier sections at the center.

Fishing Area. The surfaces of rail ends and joint bars that contact each other.

Fishing Space. The space between the head and base of a rail occupied by the joint bar.

Fish-Plate. A short piece lapping a joint, secured to the side of both members to connect them end to end.

Fishtail (Steelmaking). A condition caused by elongation variations in the ingot cross section as it is rolled into rails. The condition is normally removed in the discard of the crop end.

Fixed Signal. A signal of fixed location indicating a condition affecting the movement of a train or engine. (Standard Code)

Fixed Tube Gauging Device. A device which is attached to a tank car and which is used to determine the maximum amount of product which can be loaded into the car. It is also known as a "tell-tale."

Flag Stop. A station at which trains will stop only upon being signaled.

Flair. A tapered widening of the flangeway at the end of the guard line of a track structure, as at the end of a guard rail or at the end of a frog or crossing wing rail.

Flange (General). Any projecting surface or area, generally small with respect to the main component of which it is a part, included to serve some special purpose.

Flange (of a Wheel). The vertical projection along the inner rim of a wheel that serves, in conjunction with the flange of the mating wheel, to keep the wheel set on the track, and provides the lateral guidance system for the mounted pair.

Flanged Brake Shoes. Brake shoes so constructed that they bear on both the tread and flange of a wheel.

Flange Fittings. Special pipe fittings made with flanges held together by bolts. The joints are made tight by the use of washers or gaskets.

Flange Frog. A frog provided with guides or flanges, above its running surface, which contact the tread rims of wheels for the purpose of safely guiding their flanges past the point of the frog.

Flange Lubricator. A device by means of which either grease or oil can be applied to the flanges of a locomotive driving wheel for the purpose of preventing flange wear and cutting. Rail lubricators, mounted along the rail in high curvature territory, are also used to apply lubricant to passing flanges to reduce both wheel and rail wear.

Flanger. A form of plow, sometimes placed under a special car, called a "flanger car," but usually under a snow plow for clearing ice and snow from the inside of the rails to provide a clear passage for the wheel flanges. Flangers are also frequently attached to locomotives either on or just behind the pilot. Also called "snow scraper."

Flange Thickness. The thickness of a wheel flange, as measured along an established "baseline," from the back of the flange to a point on its front surface. A minimum limit of 15/16" is established for flange thickness on freight car wheels.

Flangeway. The open way through a track structure which provides a passageway for wheel flanges.

Flangeway Guard. A protective device that keeps the wheels in proper alignment on a railroad crossing.

Flashing. Any strip of sheet metal of an L-section used to make a water-tight joint.

Flash Point. The lowest temperature at which vapors of a volatile combustible substance ignite in air when exposed to flame.

Flatcar. A freight car having a flat floor or deck laid on the underframe, with no sides, ends or roof, designed for handling commodities not requiring protection from the weather.

Flat Car Rate (Tariff). A lump sum assessed for a carload movement instead of so much per hundredweight or ton. Such rates are usually named for switching, concentration services and short hauls (generally on carloads of coal, stone, sand, gravel and like commodities).

Flat Slab. A concrete slab having reinforcement bars extending in two or more directions without beams or girders to carry the load to supporting members.

Flat Spot. Loss of roundness of the tread of a railroad wheel caused by wheel-sliding.

Flat Switching. Switching movements in a yard where cars are moved by a locomotive on relatively level tracks as opposed to over a hump.

Flat Yard. A yard where car switching is dependent on locomotive power with little assistance from gravity.

Flemish Bond. That disposition of bricks in a structure in which the headers and stretchers alternate in each course, the header being so placed that the outer end lies on the middle of a stretcher in the course below.

Flexible Carrier. A term sometimes used to describe the spring supported coupler carrier on cars with Type F couplers.

Flexible Connection. A general term applied to the arrangement of pipes and flexible joints through which steam, air or water is conveyed in places where motion or the changing of the relative position of two points will not permit the use of rigid piping.

Flexible Joint. A joint so designed as to provide for a degree of flexibility. A ball and socket joint is an example of a flexible joint.

Flexible Truck. A truck with a flexible connection between the bolster and side frame.

Float Bridge. A structure with an adjustable apron to connect tracks on land with those on a car float, thus permitting cars to be transferred between the land and the car float at varying water levels.

Floating Battery. A storage battery maintained in operating condition by a continuous charge at low rate, or primary battery which is rectifier-coupled to receive a supplementary source of energy.

Floating Center Sill. The sliding sill portion of a cushioned underframe car.

Floating Charge. A continuous input of charging current to a storage battery.

Floating Lever. A lever used in brake rigging to equalize forces in the system.

Floor. The general term given to the layer of material which is placed on top of the underframe of a car and provides the direct support for the car contents.

Floor Beam. A beam for supporting the floor stringers and acting, to a certain extent, as a tie between the side and center sills.

Floor Height. The distance measured vertically from the top of the rail to the top surface of the floor in a railroad car.

Floor Plate. A sheet steel plate, ribbed or perforated, attached to a boxcar floor and reaching across the car from one side door to the other, to protect the floor from loading damage.

Floor Push. A circuit controller mounted in the floor so that a circuit may be made by pressing on a plunger.

Floor Rack. A rack built for use on freight car floors to accommodate certain classes of lading.

Flowed Head. The head of a rail where steel has rolled out toward the sides without showing any indication of a breaking down of the head structure.

Flow Meter. An instrument which indicates the rate of flow of a gas or liquid through a pipe, often used in connection with the testing of air brake equipment.

Flush Bolt. A spring-loaded bolt inside a slide which is attached on a door, sash or window, flush with its surface. A spring flush bolt is commonly called a "cupboard catch."

Flush Deck. Denoting the design of a long flatcar in which the side sills do not extend above the running surface of the deck.

Flush Handle. A handle for a lock or latch which is placed in a recess and which does not project beyond the surface of the object to which it is attached.

Flux. Fusable material used in soldering, welding or oxygen-cutting operations to dissolve and facilitate removal of oxides and other undesirable impurities.

Flywheel. A heavy disc or wheel mounted on an engine shaft which, through rotational inertia, resists irregular impulses of each piston thrust and produces an more even turning of the engine.

F.O.B. (Free on Board). A term employed in domestic trade to mean the delivery of goods with charges paid on board cars at some specified point such as F.O.B. Factory, or F.O.B. Shipper's dock. The term implies that shipping charges from that point on are the responsibility of the buyer of the goods.

Focal Length. The distance from the optical center of a mirror or lens at which parallel rays are brought to a focus.

Focus. A point where all the rays of light coming from a lens or mirror either meet or seem to meet.

Folding Lavatory. A wash stand for rooms in sleeping, private, and business cars which can be folded out of the way and out of sight.

Follower. A member interposed between the hammer and pile to transmit blows to the latter.

Follower (Car Construction). A steel plate or block arranged to fit inside a coupler yoke, bearing on the ends of the draft gear and transmitting the buff and draft forces from the yoke to the gear and the center sill through the draft lugs.

Follower Plate Support. A support or guide placed across the center of draft sills for the draft gear followers.

Foot Board. A step for engine crew or other personnel to ride at the front and rear of a locomotive.

Foot Guard. A filler for the space between converging rails to prevent the feet of persons from becoming accidentally wedged between the rails.

Footing. A structural unit used to distribute wall or column loads to the foundation materials.

Foot-pound. A unit of energy or work. The amount of work required to raise 1 pound a distance of 1 foot against the force of gravity.

Foreign Car. Any car not belonging to the particular railway on which it is running.

Foreign Carriers. A term used by a carrier in making reference to all other carriers collectively.

Forestall. As applied to an automatic train stop or train control device, to prevent an automatic brake application by operation of an acknowledging device or by manual control of the speed of the train. (I.C.C.)

Former Standard. A specification, design, product or device which was previously designated as Standard or Alternate Standard which has been superseded, and continues to be acceptable in interchange service, but may be subject to prescribed conditions. (A.A.R.)

Foul Bill of Lading. A bill of lading indicating that a damage or shortage existed at the time of shipment.

Fouling Point. The location on a turnout back of the frog at which insulated joints or derails are placed at or beyond clearance point.

Foundation. Any material, including piling or other special construction, which supports a structure and its load.

Foundation Brake Gear (Rigging). The complete system of levers, rods, pins, and their associated parts that serves to connect the brake cylinder piston to the brake shoes. Sometimes a distinction is made between truck brake rigging and foundation brake rigging, the former including all components from the truck live lever to the brake shoes, and the latter taken to mean all components from the cylinder lever to the fulcrum lever connecting rod. See Brake Rigging.

Four-Position Signal. A light signal unit arranged to provide four aspects.

Four-Stroke Cycle. The operating cycle of an internal combustion engine in which there is one power stroke in two revolutions of the crankshaft.

Four Way Entry. A term used to describe a safety dome platform or safety operating platform having four entrances.

FRA. See Federal Railroad Administration.

Framed Trestle. A structure in which the upright members or supports are framed timbers.

Free Lighterage. A privilege accorded shipments in car lots (domestic, export, import, coastwise and intercoastal) which are unloaded from cars and transferred to lighters and transported to and from a restricted territory within a harbor without an additional charge beyond the railhead.

Free Time. On carload freight, the time allowed to the consignor to load freight and the consignee to unload freight before demurrage charges begin to accrue. On L.C.L. freight it is the time allowed consignees before storage charges accrue.

Freight. Goods being moved from one place to another by transportation lines; also a term used to express the transportation charge.

Freight Bill. The bill, or invoice, rendered by a carrier, giving description of the freight, weight, rate, tax, whether collect or prepaid, advances and amount of charges.

Freight Car. A general term used to designate all kinds of cars which carry goods, merchandise, produce and minerals.

Freight Car Miles Per Car Day. Total freight car-miles, including loaded and empty divided by the average number of freight cars on line, including serviceable and unserviceable, divided by the number of days in the period.

Freight Car Repairs Per Freight Car Mile. Freight car repair expense divided by the sum of loaded and empty freight car miles including caboose.

Freight Charges. Charges assessed for transporting freight.

Freight Claim. A demand upon the carrier. See Claim.

Freight Forwarder. An agent who receives and forwards goods. Also, one who specializes in assembling less-than-carload freight at a central point and consolidates the same into carload lots to be forwarded to distant points.

Freight House. Another name for freight station, depot or facility of a carrier for receiving or delivering freight, usually detached from the passenger station.

Freight Rate. A charge made for transportation of freight; published in tariff form by the carriers and filed with the Interstate Commerce Commission.

Freight Receipt. A receipted freight or expense bill.

Freight Revenue. Revenue derived from freight business by transportation company.

Freight Tariff. The carrier's schedule of charges or price list, expressed in dollars and cents per 100 pounds, or per ton, etc., for the transportation and handling of freight between and at such points as are named therein, under such conditions as are in conformity with the bill of lading or the law and governed by the classification specified on title page.

Freight Train Car. A freight-carrying car, caboose, or other train service equipment required in the operation of a freight train.

Freight Truck. A freight car truck. See Truck.

Friction Casting. In freight car truck snubbing systems, the cast wheel wedge that presses against mating wear surfaces in the truck bolster and/or side frames, and serves to dampen some of the undesirable vertical motion of the bolster.

Friction Gear. A term used to refer to any draft gear utilizing friction for all or a portion of its energy-absorption capability. So-called standard draft gear cars use friction gear as opposed to hydraulic or cushioned gear which is used in cars equipped with end of car cushioning. See Cushioning, Draft Gear and End-of-Car Cushioning Device.

Friction Plate. A term sometimes used to describe a hardened steel plate which has been attached to some other softer material in an area that is exposed to conditions causing severe wear. The term "wear-plate" is more commonly used to refer to this component.

Frog. A track structure used at the intersection of two running rails to provide support for wheels and passageways for their flanges, thus permitting wheels on either rail to cross the other.

Frog Angle. The angle formed by the intersecting gage lines of a frog.

Frog Heel. The end of a frog furtherest from the switch, or the end which has both point rails or other running surfaces between the gage lines.

Frog Number. One-half the cotangent of one-half the frog angle, or the number of units of center line length in which the spread is one unit.

Frog Point. That part of a frog lying between the gage lines extending from their intersection toward the heel end.

Frog, Throat. The point at which the converging wings of a frog are closest together.

Frog, Toe. That end of a frog which is nearer the switch; or, the end which has both gage lines between the wing rail or other running surfaces.

Front End Support. A term sometimes used when referring to a piggyback trailer hitch. See Trailer Hitch.

Front Stops. The lugs fastened to the side walls of the draft sill at the front end, or end nearest the coupler, sometimes called the "front draft lugs."

Fuel. In general, the raw material used to support combustion. Virtually all non-electric locomotives in North American in main line service use a refined petroleum product as fuel for a Diesel engine.

Fuel Oil Tank. A tank for carrying a supply of fuel oil generally carried or built into the underframe of the locomotive. It is equipped with an air vent and flame arrester to prevent fires.

Fuel Pump. A unit used to transfer fuel oil from its reservoir to the locomotive engine where it is forced into the cylinders by the injector pump.

Fuel Rack. A rack which rotates the plunger of the fuel injection pump to control the amount of fuel injected into the diesel-engine cylinder. It is operated by the governor through control rods and linkage.

Fuel Saver. A type of engine; a device located in the carburetor which assists in saving fuel.

Full Crew Law. A law which specifies the number of men the carriers are required to use in connection with the operation of trains.

Fuse. A protective device installed in an electric circuit consisting of a wire strip or bar of fusible metal designed to melt and open the circuit when the current exceeds a predetermined value.

Fuse Box. A container, generally with a hinged door, containing one or more fuse receptacles with provision for ready removal and replacement of fuses.

Fusee. A warning device consisting of a cardboard tube filled with a combustible mixture of chemicals that burns brightly when ignited and remains burning for varying lengths of time. Fussees are ignited and dropped on the right-of-way to indicate to a following train the presence of stopped or slow-moving equipment ahead.

Fusion. The melting together of base metal and filler metal, or base metal only, to achieve coalescence in welding operations.

G

Gage. In general terms, any device used for measuring an independent quantity such as pressure rate of flow, volume, length, area, etc.

Gage (Track). See Standard Gage.

Gage Glass. A volume gage consisting of a clear vertical glass tube connected at the top and bottom with a tank so as to indicate the height of liquid contained in the tank.

Gage Line. A line 5/8 in. below the top of the center line of the head of running rail along that side which is nearer the center of the track.

Gage Plate. A metal plate, extending from rail to rail, used to maintain gage of track.

Gage Rod. A device for holding track to correct gage, generally consisting of 1-1/4 inch rod with a forged jaw on one end and a malleable jaw on the other end, adjustable through a locknut.

Gagging. The work done on a rail at the straightening press with a steel "gag" or tool for the purpose of taking out a bend.

Gain. A notch cut in the side of a pole to receive a cross-arm.

Galvanized. An electrolytic process by which sheet iron or steel is coated with a film of zinc to retard oxidation.

Galvanometer. An instrument or apparatus for measuring the intensity of an electric current, as well as detecting its presence or direction.

Gandy Dancer. Railroad slang for a track worker; generally regarded as derived from the track work tools made by the Gandy Mfg. Co. during the 19th century and widely used in track maintenance.

Gasket. A thin sheet of rubber, cloth, sheet metal or some other material, inserted in a joint between two mating surfaces to prevent leakage of whatever fluid is to pass through the joint.

Gas-Turbine Electric Locomotive. A locomotive in which power is developed by a gas turbine which drives electric generators supplying current to electric traction motors on the axles.

Gate. Sometimes used to describe the bottom door assembly that serves as a discharge opening on covered hopper cars, usually called the "discharge gate." In metal casting operations the gate is the opening in the mold through which the molten metal is poured.

Gateway. A point through which considerable traffic moves to or from points beyond and usually where there occurs considerable interchange between transportation lines.

Gauge. See Gage and Standard Gage.

Gear. A disc or wheel made with uniform notches around its circumference so as to form teeth that engage mating teeth on another gear to transmit torque from a driving shaft to a driven shaft.

Gear Case. An enclosure for the gear and pinion of a railway motor to exclude dirt and water.

Geared Hand Brake. A hand brake arrangement that employs gears to multiply and transmit forces applied at the hand wheel.

Gear Ratio. A pair of numbers expressed as a ratio, such as 48:12 (reads as, 48 to 12), used to describe the mechanical advantage or multiplying power of a pair of gears in a system. In the example given, the small gear (12 teeth) will turn four (4) times for every single revolution of the large gear (48 teeth), but the large gear will provide four times as much torque to its shaft as is delivered to the small gear.

General Agent. One authorized to represent his principal in all matters of a particular class.

General Freight (Merchandise). Goods offered for transport other than those commodities requiring special equipment or handling.

General Order. An order issued by authority of and over the signature of a company officer which contains changes in rules or the timetable.

Generator. A rotating electrical machine which changes mechanical energy into electrical energy. The main generator on a diesel-electric locomotive receives power from the engine and delivers electrical energy to the traction motors.

Generator Regulator. A device which controls the voltage and current output of an axle-driven electric generator to suit the needs of batteries, lights and other locomotive electrical equipment and at the same time protects the generator from injury at all train speeds.

Geotextile. A material designed to permit the passage of water through it, but not particles of soil or dirt carried by the water. Used under the ballast to function as a subballast. Also used to wrap corrugated or loose jointed pipe and to line drainage trenches or French drains. Also called "filter fabric" or "engineering fabric."

Gib. A protruding wing or guide, cast in pairs on each end of a truck bolster. The gibs form a kind of channel that fits and bears on the column guide surfaces of the side frame when the truck is assembled.

Gib and Key. A fastening to connect a bar and strap together by a slot common to both, in which a gib with a beveled back is first inserted and then driven fast by a taper key.

Gib Nut. A type of lock nut which derives its holding power from bent down edges, which, upon coming in contact with the holding nut are bent up and force the nut threads into those of the bolt to form a jam.

Girder. A type of beam used in construction, often used as the side members of a bridge.

Glad Hand. The term used to describe the metal fitting attached to the free end of each air hose. Glad hands are designed to provide for quick and positive connection of air hoses on adjacent cars.

Gland. In valve assemblies, that part of a stuffing box which surrounds the rod or stem and is pressed against the packing as the stuffing-box nut is tightened.

Gondola Car. The common gondola car is a freight car with low sides and ends, a solid floor, and no roof. It is used mainly for transportation of coal, iron and steel products and other lading not requiring protection from the weather. Special types of gondola cars are built with high sides (for coal), removable covers (for steel or aluminum coils), and other attachments for some specialized service. Some of the newer gondola cars are constructed of aluminum.

Governor (Air Brake). See Air Compressor Governor.

Governor (Locomotive). A device which controls the speed of the diesel engine and load in accordance with the throttle setting. Governor controls may be effected by electro-hydraulic, electro-pneumatic, pneumatic-hydraulic means or by mechanical linkage.

Grab Iron. See Handhold.

Grade (Noun). The ratio of the vertical change in elevation of a line with its length. For example, a 3 percent grade is a rise of 3 feet in a distance of 100 feet.

Grade (Verb). To prepare ground for construction of track or buildings.

Grade (Degree Of). As used in connection with railway line, the rise or fall in a track expressed as a ratio to 100 feet of horizontal track.

Grade Crossing. An intersection of a highway with a railroad at the same level. Also, an intersection of two or more railroad tracks at the same elevation.

Grade Line. The line on the profile representing the tops of embankments and the bottoms of cuttings ready to receive the ballast; and is the intersection of the plane of the roadbed with a vertical plane through the center line.

Gradient. The rate of inclination of the grade-line from the horizontal.

Graduated Spring. A form of compound spring in which only a certain number of the individual spirals come into action with a light load and the others only under a heavy load. Graduated springs have been superseded by single and double nest coil springs of equal length.

Graduating Valve. In air brake valves, a small slide valve fastened to the piston stem and sliding on the top of the main slide valve. It opens and closes ports in the slide valve which control the flow of air from the auxiliary reservoir to the brake cylinder in service applications, from the brake cylinder to the atmosphere in release, and also controls the quick service and quick recharge features.

Grain Door. A temporary arrangement for sealing the openings around boxcar sliding doors so that the car may be used for bulk handling of grain. One common type consists of heavy reinforced paper nailed to strips of wood which are fastened to the door posts one either side of the car door opening.

Grain Elevator. A storehouse composed of bins into which grain in bulk is stored.

Grain Line. A line marked on cars to indicate loading height for various grains.

Grain Strip. A strip of wood or other material used to prevent leakage of grain from freight cars.

Grating. A flat surface formed by welding thin steel strips on edge in a crisscross grid pattern which permits water drainage while forming a solid support for the foot. Grating sections are used for end platforms, brake steps, running boards and other applications to improve safety while walking or standing on equipment.

Green Eye (Slang). Clear signal.

Grids. Resistances introduced in electric circuits to convert electrical energy into heat, thereby controlling the current in the circuit.

Grille. A fine grating made of wire mesh or other similar material for covering openings in air ducts, or to provide protection around machinery.

Grooved Tie. A cross tie which has had grooves machined across its top depressions into which ribs on the bottom of the time plate may fit.

Groove Weld. A type of weld where the metal deposit fills a groove prepared in advance to facilitate making the joint.

Gross Earnings. Earnings of a carrier for the transportation of persons and property before deducting the costs of providing the service.

Gross Ton-Miles. A measure of transportation, being the movement of the combined weight of cars and lading a distance of one mile.

Gross Weight. The total combined weight of the car and its contents. See Light Weight and Load Limit.

Ground. An electrical connection, whether intentional or accidental, between the positive side of an electric circuit and the earth, or some conducting object that serves in its plane, such as a locomotive underframe.

Ground Detector. A device for indicating a ground on an electrical circuit.

Ground Relay. A protective device that functions to prevent operation of a locomotive in the event of a short circuit or ground in the electrical equipment. This is done to ensure the safety of the crew on the locomotive and to prevent damaging the locomotive itself.

Ground Wire. A wire connected to a ground.

Group Rate. A freight rate applicable to a large number of related points or to a definite section of territory.

Group Retarder. A retarder which is so located that it is the last retarder the cars pass through before going into a single group of classification tracks.

Grouping (of Wood for Ties). Sorting forest products into groups according to their sapwood content, size, strength, and treatability.

Grout. A fluid mixture of cement and water or of cement, sand and water, with or without admixture.

Guard Brace. A metal shape designed to fit the contour of the side of the guard rail and extend over the tie, with provision for fastening thereto, to restrain the moving or tilting of the guard rail away from the running rail.

Guard Check Gage. The distance between guard line and gage line, measured across the track at right angles to the gage lines.

Guard Clamp. A device consisting of a yoke and fastenings designed to engage the running rail and the guard rail and hold them in correct relation to each other.

Guard Face Gage. The distance between guard lines, measured across the track at right angles to the gage lines.

Guard Line. A line along that side of the flangeway which is nearer the center of the track and at the same elevation as the gage line.

Guard Rail. A rail or other structure laid parallel with the running rails of a track to prevent wheels from being derailed; or to hold wheels in correct alignment to prevent their flanges from striking the points of turnout or crossing frogs or the points of switches.

Guard Timber. A longitudinal timber placed outside of the track rail, to maintain the spacing of ties.

Guide Rails. Longitudinal members extending along the deck of a flatcar to restrain lateral movement and guide the wheels of automotive vehicles while moving during loading and unloading operations.

Gun Iron. A tough, close-grained and strong cast iron, made of special mixtures, including steel scrap. Used for piston rings and parts requiring strength or subjected to wear.

Gusset Plate. A flat steel plate used to reinforce a joint between two members in a steel structure.

Guy. A tension member having one end secured to a fixed object and the other end attached to a pole, crossarm, or other structural part that it surrounds.

H

Hand Brake. A device mounted on railway cars and locomotives to provide a means for applying brakes manually without air pressure. Common types include vertical wheel, horizontal wheel and lever type, so named because of the configuration or orientation of their operating handles.

Hand Brake Chain. The chain which forms part of the connection between the hand brake shaft and the brake levers.

Hand Brake Housing. An enclosure containing the gearing and release mechanism of a hand brake.

Hand Brake Wheel. A steel hand wheel, approximately 14 inches in diameter, attached to the brake shaft to provide a means for manually applying the brakes.

Hand Car. A four-wheeled car used in connection with track inspection and repair work by maintenance employees for transporting men, tools, etc. Most hand cars are powered by gasoline or electricity instead of manually.

Handhold. A round steel bar of 5/8" minimum diameter, formed with a means for mechanical attachment to a car side, end or roof, to provide a secure place for crewmen to hold on to the equipment. Handholds are considered "safety appliances" by the FRA, and as such, are subject to very strict regulations with respect to placement and clearances. Also known as "grab irons."

Handhole. A small opening in a crankcase, tank or other vessel usually provided with air and water tight seal which can be removed so that the hand may be inserted for making repairs or for other purposes.

Handrail. A bar or rail to be grasped with the hand.

Hand Rail Post. A support for the hand rail.

Hanger. Any component of a mechanical system that serves to support other components in the system by suspension. The use of the term hanger generally implies that the parts are suspended at pinned connections, and are free to move as the mechanism may require.

Hasp. A slotted bar that fits over a U-shaped staple forming a connection that can be secured with a pin or wedge driven through the staple in front of the hasp.

Hatch. The opening through which products are loaded in covered hopper cars.

Hatch Cover. The hinged door that closes and seals a hatch on the roof of a covered hopper car.

Haul. To transport by drawing. Usually, the term denotes that significant weight is involved.

Hazardous Material. When used with respect to lading in transportation vehicles, a term identifying the lading as subject to specific safety requirements set forth by the Department of Transportation and/or the Interstate Commerce Commission. Examples of hazardous materials are explosives, poisons, flammable liquids, corrosive substances, and oxidizing or radioactive materials.

H-Beam. A wide flange rolled structural beam having a cross section similar to the letter "H".

Head Block Signal. A home signal governing entrance into the block between sidings on single track.

Head-End Power. A system of furnishing electric power for a complete railway train from a single generating plant either in the locomotive or on a special power car.

Head Rod. A rod connecting the points of a switch or movable point frog, by means of which the relative location of the points is maintained and to which the operating rod is attached.

Head Shield. A supplemental heavy steel plate required by federal regulation on the ends of some hazardous commodity tank cars to lessen the chances of tank head puncture by the coupler of an adjacent car in the event of excessive end impact or derailment. Head shields can be either "full" (covering the entire end of the tank) or "partial" (covering only the lower portion of the tank head).

Head Ties. The ties to which a switch stand is attached.

Heat Balance. A tabulation showing the heat developed by combustion in the engine cylinder that is: delivered in the form of power at the crankshaft; lost in friction; lost to the cooling water; and lost in the exhaust gases.

Heater Car. A car equipped with heating apparatus for carrying fruit, vegetables and other products during cold weather.

Also, a car fitted with a steam generator for heating of passenger trains.

Heater Piped Car. A tank car equipped with either exterior or interior heater coils in which steam is applied at an unloading point to facilitate the liquefying of viscous or semi-solid lading thus permitting normal unloading. This type of tank car is referred to as an HP car or an IHP car if it is insulated.

Heat Treatment. The process of altering the properties of a material, usually steel, by specific heating and cooling operations.

Heavy Duty, Car. A self-propelled car weighing from 1,400 to 2,000 lbs. or more, and designed for hauling trailers and such other equipment as ballast diskers and weed mowers; it is also used for hump yard service. Seats and decks may be lengthened to accommodate a large work crew. It is propelled by engines ranging from 12 to 30 hp.

Heavy Repairs. As reported to the Association of American Railroads, repairs to revenue freight cars requiring over 20 man-hours.

Heavy Section. A motor car (1,200 - 1,400 lbs.) with a seating capacity for 10 to 12 men, usually equipped with 8 to 12 hp. engines. Used largely with large section or extra gangs. Also may haul one or more trailers with men and tools.

Heel (of Frog). The end of a frog farthest from the switch.

Heel (of Switch). The end of a switch rail farthest from the point of a switch.

Heel Block. A steel block through which bolt holes are drilled which is placed between the heel of a switch point and its stick rail.

Helical Spring. A spring made of bar steel wound in a coil to form a helix. Standard truck springs are helical springs, but are more commonly known as "coil springs."

Helper Locomotive. A locomotive usually placed towards the rear of a train, to assist in the movement of the train over heavy grades. Helper locomotives can be either manned, or remotely controlled from the lead unit in the train.

Hi-Cube Car. A term used to describe any of a series of boxcars whose inside dimensions are such as to produce a cubic capacity of approximately 10,000 cu. ft., as opposed to the cube of conventional cars, which is usually in the range of 4,000 to 6,000 cu. ft.

High and Wide. A term referring to outside dimensions of a car or open top load that exceed the normal clearances on the route to be traveled.

Hi-Hat. A term used to identify that portion of the draft gear housing on low level piggyback and auto rack flatcars that extends above the deck of the car. Also, the configuration of the upper surface of one design of plain journal bearing.

High Side Gondola Car. A gondola car, with sides and ends over 36 in. high, for carrying coal or minerals.

Highball. Signal given to proceed at maximum authorized speed. The word originated from earlier railroad practice of hoisting a ball on a pulley to show that the track ahead was clear.

Hinge. A joint between two members so constructed as to allow one or both of the members to pivot upon a common axis. The axis is generally a pin passing through a series of cylindrical eyes fastened to each member and brought into a common alignment.

Hinge Pin. The bolt or pin about which the two members of a hinged joint pivot.

Hi-Rail (Noun). A truck or automobile with retractable flanged wheels so it may be used on either highway or track. Also called "hi-railer."

Hold Clear. A term used to designate a device for holding a signal in any position other than its most restrictive.

Hold Track. A track in a storage yard where cars are held, awaiting disposition orders by consignees or owners.

Hollow Rod. The piston rod of a standard freight car brake cylinder, so named because it is made hollow to receive the cylinder push rod.

Home Junction. A junction with the home road.

Home Point. A specified location on a railroad which, by agreement, is considered as a home junction for cars belonging to non-railroad private car owners.

Home Road. For any car, the home road is the railroad that owns the car.

Home Route. The line of intermediate roads over which a foreign car was moved to or from its home road.

Home Signal. A fixed signal at the entrance of a route or block to govern trains or engines entering and using that route or block. (Standard Code)

Hook Bolt. A bolt having a hook-shaped end instead of the conventional head.

Hook and Eye Brake. A term used to describe a relatively new foundation brake arrangement where the truck levers are formed with a hook at one end that connects to an eye welded to the end of the mating brake rod. This arrangement replaces the conventional clevis and pin connection. The arrangement was developed to accommodate close clearance conditions between the truck and body bolsters on freight cars with large center plates and sliding sill cushioning. The concept has subsequently spread to other types of cars, and the arrangement is becoming more common.

Hopper Car. A freight car, either open or covered, designed for handling bulk commodities such as coal or grain. Hopper cars have floor sheets that slope from the car sides and ends to form a series of pockets, or hoppers, which when opened, can discharge the bulk lading by gravity through hopper doors operated from outside the car.

Hopper Door. A door at the bottom of the hopper on hopper cars which when opened permits rapid discharge of bulk lading either between or outside of the rails depending on the type of door design. Hopper doors on covered hopper cars are often known as "discharge gates."

Horizontal Split Head. A horizontal progressive defect originating inside of the rail head, usually 1/4 inch or more below the running surface and progressing horizontally in all directions, and generally accompanied by a flat spot on the running surface. The defect appears as a crack lengthwise of the rail when it reaches the side of the rail head. See Compound Fissure.

Horizontal Wheel Hand Brake. A type of hand brake incorporating a vertical brake staff and a horizontally mounted brake wheel as opposed to a vertically mounted geared hand brake or a side mounted brake with a pump type handle.

Horsepower. A unit of power equivalent to 33,000 foot-pounds per minute or 746 watts.

Hose. Tubing made of rubber and canvas or other flexible materials, used to convey a fluid, generally over relatively short distances. See Air Hose.

Hose Clamp. A clamp or collar to bind the hose to the hose nipple of coupling. Sometimes called a "hose band."

Hose Coupling. See Glad Hand.

Hose Nipple. A short iron tube fitting into the end of the air brake hose and fastened by a suitable clamp. One end is threaded and screws into the angle cock.

Hostler. A person who operates light engines in designated enginehouse territory and works under the direction of the enginehouse foreman.

Hostler's Control. A simplified throttle provided to move a diesel locomotive unit not equipped with a regular engineer's control.

Hotbed. A series of skids on which rails are placed for cooling after rolling, sawing and cambering.

Hot Box. Railroad slang for an overheated journal bearing.

Hot Box Detector. A heat sensitive device installed along railroad mainline track at strategic locations for measuring the relative temperatures of passing journal bearings. Bearing temperatures are transitted to wayside stations and are monitored by personnel who can act to stop a train if an overheated journal is discovered. Some hot box detectors will automatically drop the next block signal to a stop indication if an overheated condition is noted, thus, stopping the train to allow for an inspection.

House Track. A track alongside or entering a freight house, used for cars receiving or delivering freight at the house.

Housing. A term frequently applied to any part which encases some or all of the working parts of a machine.

HST. Abbreviation for "high speed train."

Hub. The central portion of a wheel into which the axle is fitted.

Hump. The hill over which cars are pushed for classification in a hump yard.

Humping Speed. A term generally used in classification yards to denote the rate at which cars are pushed over the apex of a hump for classification. Humping speed is usually expressed either in terms of cars per minute or miles per hour. Four cars per minute is equivalent to 2.04 miles per hour, using an average car length of 45 feet.

Hump Repeater Signal. A signal that repeats the hump-signal indication, used where the hump signal is not visible to the engine crew.

Hump Signal. A signal located near the summit in a hump yard which gives indication concerning movement to the classification tracks and indicates to the engineman the desired direction and speed of movement of his train.

Hump Signal Controller. A device located at the hump which includes the hump signal control lever and may also include the trimmer signal control lever and signal repeater lights.

Hump Signal Emergency Lever. A lever usually located in one of the control towers and used to operate electric contacts that control the hump-signal circuit to set up stop indication on the hump signal, the trimmer signal, and the repeater signals when in an emergency the operator desires to stop operation.

Hump Speed Control. A lever designated F-N-S or hump modification plus-minus potentiometer used in connection with speed control systems applied to classification yards. These controls are located on retarder control panels to allow the operator to pre-select speeds for either fast, normal or slow operation to compensate for car rolling characteristics as influenced by conditions such as weather, etc.

Hump Yard. A railroad classification yard in which the classification of cars is accomplished by pushing them over a summit, known as a "hump," beyond which they run by gravity.

Hydraulic Jack. A jack in which the power is exerted by means of the pressure of some liquid acting against a piston or plunger. See Jack.

Hydropneumatic Brake. A braking system for railroad cars that utilizes compressed air to control the action of a hydraulic piston that ultimately applies braking force to the wheels. Braking control can be transmitted from car to car in the conventional way, while the advantages of hydraulics can be employed to actually apply the brakes without the rigging problems inherent in conventional foundation gear.

I

I-Beam. A general term applied to any form of rolled steel having a cross section the shape of a capital "I". The top and bottom parts are termed the flanges and the middle the web.

I.C.C. Abbreviation for Interstate Commerce Commission.

Icing. Placing ice in bunkers of a refrigerator car prior to and/or during transportation for the purpose of preserving commodities requiring protection against heat.

I.D. A term used when referring to the inside diameter of a cylinder or any circular surface such as the bore of a railway car wheel.

Idle. The speed at which an engine turns over when it is not under load.

Idle Hour System. A method of furnishing empty cars to coal mines whereby the allotment is reduced or increased according to the level of utilization in comparison with other mines.

Idler Car. Usually a flatcar used in the transportation of a long article or shipment, which extends beyond the limits of the car carrying the shipment; the "idler" being a car on which the shipment or article does not rest, but overhangs.

IDT. Initials that stand for "in-date-test," periodic test of the air brake equipment on every car to assure its continued proper operation. The month, day and year of the most recent IDT must be stenciled on every car.

Ignition. The burning of fuel oil within the combustion chamber of a cylinder. In a Diesel engine, this is accomplished by compressing the air in each cylinder, with the heat of compression being sufficient to ignite the fuel.

Ignitron. High voltage, high current mercury vapor (pool-type) rectifier which is gated by a pulse applied to its starting electrode (ignitor). Ignitron rectifiers were used in some electric locomotives.

Impact Tests. A standard series of controlled and instrumented test couplings of cars at increasingly higher speeds to determine the effect of switching impacts on the car frame structure and lading with respect to various draft arrangements on the cars under test.

Impedance. The apparent resistance in a electric circuit to the flow of an alternating current, analogous to the actual electrical resistance to a direct current.

Impedance Bond. As used on electrified railroads, an iron core coil of low-resistance and relatively high reactance to provide a continuous path for the return propulsion current around insulated joints and to confine the alternating-current signaling energy to its own track circuit.

Incising. Puncturing the longitudinal surfaces of poles, ties, and timbers to assure penetration by a preservative and to relieve surface tension as an aid in the control of checking.

Incline. An inclined track or tracks and their supporting structure.

In-Date-Test. See IDT.

Independent Brake. The air brake control valve on a locomotive unit that controls the brakes on that locomotive (or multiple unit consist) independently from the train brakes.

Independent Pressure Switch. A device installed on a locomotive that will automatically cut-out the extended range dynamic braking when an independent brake application of sufficient magnitude is made, usually 15 psi. This is to prevent the wheels of the locomotive from sliding due to excessive braking forces.

Induced Current. A current produced in a secondary circuit by change in the current of a primary circuit.

Industrial Car. A railway car used primarily in intraplant service for moving such material as steel billets, hot metal, sand or other rough commodities. Industrial cars are not suitable for interchange service and are exempt from provisions of the FRA Safety Standards.

Industrial Line. A short railroad owned by one or more of the industries using it.

Industrial Track. A switching track serving industries, such as mines, mills, smelters, and factories.

Inertia. A term used in the study of physics to describe the natural tendency of a body to maintain its existing velocity.

Inert Retarder. A braking device, without external power, built into a railway track to reduce the speed of cars by means of brake shoes against the sides of the lower portions of the wheels and sometimes provided with means for opening it to nullify its braking effect.

Inflatable Bulkhead. A special type of load divider consisting of two or three vertical bulkheads separated by inflatable air bags that can expand and exert a controlled longitudinal force against the lading, thus preventing undesired movement during transit. See Load Divider.

Initial Air. The forcing of compressed air into wood in a treating cylinder just prior to adding the preservative and maintained at the desired pressure during the filling of the cylinder.

Initial Charge. A term used in expressing the first charge given a storage battery after it has been set-up, also to designate the recommended current applied to electrical apparatus at the beginning of a series of tests.

Initial Terminal. The starting point of a locomotive for a trip.

Injector. The pump and nozzle used to force fuel oil into a cylinder under great pressure.

Inspection Car. A car used for inspecting track and right-of-way.

Instruction Car. A car used for the instruction of railway employees in matters pertaining to their work.

Instrument Panel. The board upon which various gages are mounted, electrical, air, oil, etc.

Insulated Rail Joint. A joint in which electrical insulation is provided between adjoining rails. (I.C.C.)

Insulation (Car Construction). In general, any material that serves to decrease the flow of heat through a structural wall from one space to another. Common insulating materials in rail car applications include polyurethane foam and fiber glass, both used in refrigerator cars. Dead air space between wall panels also serves as effective insulation.

Insulation (Electrical). Any material that prevents the flow of electric current from one conductor to another, or to the ground.

Intake. That portion of a pipe or other apparatus through which water, air, or other fluid enters from the source of supply.

Interchange. The transfer of cars from one road to another at a common junction point.

Interchange Point. The geographical point, yard, junction, or track common to two railroads where cars are routinely interchanged from one railroad to another.

Interchange Rules. A set of regulations adopted by the Association of American Railroads governing the care and handling of freight cars operating in interchange service. The Interchange Rules are contained in two publications known as the Field Manual and the Office Manual, and are revised and reissued annually to meet changing conditions.

Interchange Track. A track on which cars are delivered, or received, as between railways.

Intercooler. A heat exchanger interposed between the low-pressure and high-pressure stages of the air compressor. By reducing the temperature of the air at the intake of the high-pressure stage the volumetric efficiency of the compressor is improved.

Interior Heater. A term used to describe any of several tank car heating systems using pipes or coils mounted on the inside of the tank and in direct contact with the fluid to be heated. See Exterior Heater Pipes.

Interline Freight. Tonnage passing over the lines of two or more carriers. The interchange between the carriers is termed an "interline movement."

Interlock. Electrical contacts mounted on other contactors, unit switches or the reverser so that they are opened or closed as the contactor, unit switch or reverser operates. Closing the main contacts may either open or close the interlock contacts and vice versa.

Interlocking. An arrangement of signals and signal appliances so interconnected that their movements must succeed each other in proper sequence and for which interlocking rules are in effect. It may be operated manually or automatically. (Standard Code)

Interlocking, Automatic. An arrangement of signals, with or without other signal appliances, which functions automatically as distinguished from those functions are controlled manually, and which are so interconnected by means of electric circuits that their movements must succeed each other in proper sequence, train movements over all routes being governed by signal indication.

Interlocking Limits. The tracks between the home signals of an interlocking. (Standard Code)

Interlocking Machine. An assemblage of manually operated levers or equivalent devices, for the control of signals, switches or other units, and including mechanical or circuit locking or both to establish proper sequence of movements.

Interlocking, Manual. An arrangement of signals and signal appliances operated from an interlocking machine and so interconnected by means of mechanical and/or electric locking that their movements must succeed each other in proper sequence, train movements over all routes being governed by signal indication. (I.C.C.)

Interlocking Plants. Generally taken to mean the building and equipment located within the interlocking limits and used in the operation of the interlocking.

Interlocking Signals. The fixed home signals of an interlocking.

Interlocking Station. A place from which an interlocking is operated. (Standard Code)

Intermediate Carrier. With respect to movement of a specific car, the intermediate carrier moves the car over its lines from and to interchange with other carriers, but neither originates or terminates the traffic. Sometimes known as a "bridge carrier."

Intermodal Car. A rail car designed specifically for handling piggyback trailers or containers, or both. Intermodal cars may be long flatcars with collapsable trailer hitches, or shorter, lightweight platforms with rigid hitches for use at mechanized terminals. Some newer designs are articulated, and have as many as ten platforms connected to form one "car."

Intermodal Traffic. Freight moving via at least two different modes of transport.

Internal Combustion Engine. An engine in which power is obtained by the combustion of a gaseous or liquid fuel in a series of cylinders.

Interstate Commerce. Movement of goods from one state to another.

Interstate Commerce Act. Comprises the original Act to Regulate Commerce (approved Feb. 4, 1887), and many other amendments. It is now in four parts: Part I relating to regulation of railroads and common carriers in general, Part II to motor carriers, Part III to water carriers, and Part IV to freight forwarders.

Inter-Terminal Switching. An interchange of cars, the movement of which is confined to the switching limits of the same station or switching district.

Intra-Plant Switching. The movement of cars from one place to another within the yards of a plant or industry.

Intra-Terminal Switching. The movement of cars from one place to another within the limits of a terminal on the same transportation line.

Island Platform. A passenger platform separated from the buildings or main platform, usually on the opposite side of main-line tracks from the station, or often constructed between tracks.

Isolation Switch. An electrical device in a Diesel electric locomotive which disconnects the controls of the locomotive from the cab control circuits. The switch must be in the "RUN" position in order for the unit to develop power.

J

Jack. A mechanical device for lifting heavy objects by applying the required force from beneath the object. The necessary force is commonly obtained either by a long lever arm (with a ratchet arrangement), by a screw or with air or hydraulic pressure.

Jacket. A thin outer shell over a tank or pipe, often made of sheet metal, and used to contain insulating material wrapped around the pipe or tank.

Jacking Pads. Heavy steel pads attached to car side sills at each corner near the bolster, and designed to support the weight of the car on jacks.

Jackknife. A term used to describe an extremely adverse condition existing between two rail vehicles (or a highway tractor and its trailer) whereby excessive sharp angularity occurs at the pivoting connection between the two units, resulting in severe misalignment of the connection, and generally, in the case of rail cars, a derailment. Jackknifing is caused by excessively high buff forces in a train.

Jaw. A forked attachment used for making a pivotal connection. Also, the part of a wrench, vise, or other holding mechanism that contacts the piece or pieces to be clamped.

Jaw Bolt. A bolt with a forked end instead of the conventional head.

Joint Bar. A steel bar commonly used in pairs for joining rail ends in railroad track.

Joint Facility. Railway property which two or more carriers either own, maintain or operate by formal agreement for this common benefit.

Joint Gap. The distance between the ends of contiguous rails in track, measured at a point 5/8 in. below the top of the rail on the outside of the head.

Joint Rate. A joint rate is one agreed upon by two or more carriers and applies between a point on the line of one and a point on the line of another. Such a rate may include one or more intermediate lines of railroad in its route.

Joint Tariff. A schedule containing joint rates.

Joint Tie. A crosstie used under a rail joint.

Journal. The part of a railcar axle on which the journal bearing rests or is mounted.

Journal Bearing. The general term used to describe the load bearing arrangement at the ends of each axle of a railcar truck. So called plain journal bearings are blocks of metal, usually brass or bronze, shaped to fit the curved surface of the axle journal, and resting directly upon it with lubrication provided by free oil contained in the journal box. Journal roller bearings are sealed assemblies of rollers, races, cups and cones pressed onto axle journals and generally lubricated with grease. Vertical loads are transferred from the journal bearing to the truck side frame through the journal bearing wedge (in plain bearing designs), or through the roller bearing adaptor in roller bearing trucks.

Journal Bearing Wedge. A device used to hold the journal bearing in place in the journal box and to distribute the load evenly over the bearing.

Journal Box. The metal housing on a plain bearing truck which encloses the journal of a car axle, the journal bearing and wedge, and which holds the oil and lubricating device.

Journal Box Lid. A door or lid covering an opening in the journal box through which oil is added, the lubricator is inspected and serviced, and journal bearings are inserted or removed. Journal box lids are generally held closed by a strong spring.

Journal Box Seals. Devices for retaining oil and excluding water and solid contaminants from plain bearing journal assemblies. This involves a rear seal which fits in the dust guard well of the truck side frame and a front seal which fits around the edges of the journal box lid.

Journal Brass. Another term sometimes used when referring to a plain journal bearing.

Journal Jack. A small jack used for relieving the weight from car journals for the purpose of changing bearings.

Journal Lubricator. A device installed in a journal box that enables oil in the box to be evenly distributed to the bearing surfaces of the axle journal and the journal bearing for efficient lubrication of the assembly.

Journal Spring. A spring supporting part of the weight of a car which is placed directly over the journal, and which usually rests on the journal box under the truck frame.

Journal Stops. Metal castings, usually of bronze, fastened to the inside of the journal box which limit movement of the axle journal, particularly during switching impacts and brake applications.

Jumbo. A name commonly applied to the car record, when maintained on large sheets in binders, affording space for posting daily movement of fifty cars for thirty-one days to a page.

Jumper. A flexible cable, composed of one or more independently insulated conductors and fitted with plugs at each end to allow for connection of electric circuits between coupled locomotives or cars.

Junction. A point at which two or more carriers interchange freight. Also, a point where two lines of a railroad meet, usually with provision for operating trains from one line to the other.

Junction Box. In electrical circuits, a metal housing placed in a convenient location for the purpose of gaining access to otherwise concealed wiring, and providing protection for electrical connections made between conductors in the circuit.

Junction Report. In car service, a report of the delivery of a car to a connecting line; such report being made to the car owner as well as to reporting line's customary officials. See Wheel Report.

K

Keeper. A mechanical device whose function is either to prevent undesired movement of some other component, or to prevent the accidental disengagement of a lock or bolt.

Key. A mechanical device, which in various ways can be used to maintain a fixed relationship between two components in an assembly.

Key Bolt. A bolt slotted near the end to receive a key which takes the place of a nut.

Key Slot. The slot or slots in the coupler butt and draft sills through which the draft key is inserted.

Keyway. A machined slot in a shaft or in the hub of a wheel, the purpose of which is to accept a machined steel bar or key which is driven into the keyway to prevent undesired rotating of the shaft relative to the wheel.

Kicker. A slang term used by operating crews to describe a freight car whose air brake equipment is malfunctioning to produce undesired emergency brake applications in a train.

Kilowatt Hour. A unit of energy measured equal to the continuous flow of one kilowatt (1000 watts) for one hour.

Kinetic Energy. A term used in the study of physics to describe the energy contained in a moving body by virtue of its motion. The kinetic energy of a moving body is equal to the energy needed to bring it to rest.

Kingpin. On a highway semi-trailer, the short flanged steel pin projecting downward from the front load bearing surface of the underframe, which is grasped by the tractor in highway operation, or by the trailer hitch when the trailer is being transported on a piggyback flatcar.

Kitchen Car. A car provided with cooking facilities but with no provision for table service. Usually operated next to a dining car.

Knee Brace. A stiffening piece used to reinforce two members of a structure that meet at right angles.

Knuckle. The pivoting hook-like casting that fits into the head of a coupler and rotates about a vertical pin to either the open position (to engage a mating coupler) or to the closed position (when fully engaged). Coupler knuckles must conform to a standard dimensional contour specified by the Association of American Railroads.

Knuckle Pin. The steel pin holding the knuckle in the head of the coupler. The knuckle pin is sometimes known as the "knuckle pivot pin" or simply "the pivot pin."

Knuckle Rail. A bent rail, or equivalent, forming the obtuse point against which the movable center points of a movable point crossing or slip switch rest when set for traffic.

Knuckle Thrower. A device that serves to open the coupler knuckle when the uncoupling lever is operated.

L

"L" Side. That side of a rail car on the left side of the observer when facing the "B" end of the car.

Ladder. Bars of iron or steel attached by bolts or rivets to the side or end of a freight car or caboose so as to form steps by which persons may climb to and from the car. The individual bars are termed "ladder rounds."

Ladder Bolt. A bolt designed especially for securing the ladder rounds at the corner post when two rounds are directly in line on the side and end of the car.

Ladder Track. A track connecting successively the body tracks of a yard.

Lading. Another term for the load in a rail car.

Lading Strap Anchors. Tie down devices welded to structural members of a freight car and designed to accept steel banding or wire used to secure loads in or on the car.

Lagging. Strips of sheeting used to transfer weight or pressure to centering or other supporting members, commonly used in construction of tunnels, arches and shafts.

Lag Screw. A metal bolt with a square or hexagonal head but with a wood screw thread; intended to screw into wood or other soft material.

Lamp Adapter. A device that permits an electric lamp equipped with one style base to be used in a different style socket.

Lamp Bracket. A support designed to assure that the proper alignment of lamp can be maintained.

Lands. The portions of the piston between the gooves carrying the piston rings.

Lap. A surface defect on metal appearing as a seam caused from folding over hot metal, fins, or sharp corners and then rolling or forging.

Lap Joint. In welding processes, any joint formed by two overlapping members.

Lateral Motion. Sideways movement of a railcar and/or its components, resulting in large measure from dimensional clearances between parts of the truck assembly. Excessive lateral motion in truck assemblies is a major cause of premature wear of the truck and car body components.

Layshaft. A shaft extending the length of a locomotive diesel engine on both sides used to control fuel injection in each cylinder of the engine.

L.C.L. Initials meaning "less than carload" to describe a freight moving quantities of less than a carload.

Lead Curve. The curve in a turnout interposed between the switch and the frog.

Leads. Electrical cables extending out of a motor or generator with provision for connection to other apparatus.

Lead Track. An extended track connecting either end of a yard with the main track.

Lead Unit. The first and controlling unit in a locomotive consist.

Leakage Groove. A small short passage past the brake piston to prevent application of the brakes by a small leakage of air.

Leased Car. A car rented by a shipper or a carrier for a through movement.

Ledger Value. The amount at which property is carried in the Investment in Road and Equipment account.

Lens. A glass or similar product, usually circular in shape, designed to collect the rays of light directly from a light source and focus them into a beam of definite shape depending upon the design. It may be clear or colored as required.

Lessee. An individual or a corporation who has the right of use of something of value, gained through a lease agreement with the real owner of the property. Very often railroads lease car equipment from financial institutions, and this fact may be indicated on the car by stenciling, naming the owner and identifying the railroad as the lessee.

Less-Than-Carload (LCL). A term applicable to a quantity of freight which is less than the amount necessary to constitute a carload.

Less-Than-Carload Rate. A rate applicable to less than a carload shipment.

Level. The condition of the track in which the elevation of the two rails transversely is the same.

Level Board. A tool used to measure the difference in cross level elevation of the track.

Lever. One of the basic groups of simple machines consisting of a bar of rigid material used in conjunction with a support called a fulcrum. Depending on the placement of the fulcrum, the lever can be used either to: increase applied force at the expense of speed; increase speed at the expense of force; change the direction of an applied force; or to effect a combination of these advantages. The most familiar example of the lever in car construction is found in the foundation brake gear. See Brake Lever.

Lever Guide. A support and guide for a brake lever in the brake rigging.

Leverman. A title sometimes applied to the operator of an interlocking machine.

Lever-Operated Locking. The mechanical locking of an interlocking machine which is actuated by means of the lever. (I.C.C.)

Lightning Arrester. A device for protecting electrical apparatus from damage by lighting by providing a path to ground around the protected equipment.

Light Repairs. As reported to the Association of American Railroads, repairs to revenue freight cars requiring 20 man-hours or less.

Light Weight. The empty weight of a railroad car including its trucks and any other appurtenances considered standard to the car. The light weight is stenciled on every freight car in conjunction with the capacity and load limit stenciling, and is abbreviated LT. WT.

Limited Speed. A speed defined in the timetable in connection with signal indications.

Limit Gage. A term applied to many forms of gages which are used for determining whether pieces exceed or fall below a certain specified range of dimensions. Limit gages are sometimes called "Go-No Go Gages."

Line. The condition of the track with regard to uniformity in direction over short distances on tangents, or uniformity of curvature over short distances on curves.

Line Haul. The movement over the tracks of a carrier from one city to another, not including the switching service.

Line Rail. The rail on which alignment is based.

Liner (Diesel Engine). The removable inner sleeve of the engine cylinder which contacts the piston rings.

Lining. As used in boxcar construction, a thin sheathing of wood or other material applied to the inside walls and ends of closed type cars to provide a smooth, obstruction-free interior for loading. As used in tank or covered hopper car construction, a chemical coating usually in liquid form that is sprayed or foamed onto the interior surfaces of the car body to impart some desirable property to the surfaces in contact with the lading.

Lining Bar. A straight steel bar designed to be used for shifting and moving track and rails.

Link and Pin Coupler. An old type of connection between cars which employed a link and a pin arrangement.

Live Lever. Any lever in the foundation or truck brake rigging that does not have a fixed (non-movable) connection.

Live Load. In car design, the live load is the load imposed on the car structure by outside forces such as the lading and any other specified supplemental loads such as accelerations due to vertical irregularities in the track structure. See Dead Load.

Load. A measure of the output of an engine.

Load Brake Cylinder. The brake cylinder of the empty-and-load freight brake equipment that operates to increase the braking force only when the car is loaded.

Load Divider. A device installed in a closed car for the purpose of providing restraint against undesired longitudinal movement of the lading. Load dividers are generally used in pairs, and are adjustable to allow for tight placement against the lading in each end of the car.

Loaded Car Miles. Miles run by freight cars loaded with revenue or non-revenue freight.

Load Limit. The maximum weight of lading that can be loaded in a car. For cars meeting standard A.A.R. design criteria, the load limit is equal to the maximum allowable gross weight on the rails (determined by axle and wheel size), less the light weight of the car. Load limit is stenciled on every freight car in conjunction with the capacity and light weight stenciling and is abbreviated LD. LMT.

Load Meter. The ammeter at the engineer's control stand used to indicate the amount of current passing through the traction motors.

Load Regulator (or Load Pot). A potentiometer or rheostat hydraulically positioned by the locomotive governor which controls the load on the traction generator.

Local Service. The service rendered by a "local" train which stops to deliver and receive freight at each station along the route.

Location (Trackwork). The established position of the center line and grade line of a railroad preparatory to its construction.

Lock. Any device the function of which is to secure other adjacent or connecting parts in a fixed position.

Lock Bolt. A fastener used in car construction which is formed into a cold rivet by mechanical force.

Lock, Facing Point. A mechanical lock for a switch, derail or movable point frog, comprising a plunger stand and a plunger which engages a lock rod attached to the switch point to lock the operated unit.

Locking Bed. That part of an interlocking machine that contains or holds the tappets, locking bars, cross-locking, dogs, and other apparatus used to interlock the levers.

Locking Center Pin. A center pin so made as to provide a positive non-separable connection between the carbody and truck center plates.

Locking Face. The locking surface of a locking dog, tappet or cross-locking of an interlocking machine. (I.C.C.)

Lock Lifter. See Coupler Lock Lifter.

Lock Nut. A special type of nut having a feature which prevents the nut from turning off the bolt once it is secured. Lock nuts are not reusable since their removal generally destroys the locking feature.

Lock Rod. A rod, attached to the front rod or lug of a switch, movable point frog, or derail, through which a locking plunger may extend when the switch points or derail are in the normal or reverse position. (I.C.C.)

Lock Seal. A piece of material (glass, lead or paper) which forms a seal for a lock so that it cannot be opened without the seal being broken and the act discovered.

Lock Washer. A washer designed to prevent undesired loosening of a nut after it has been tightened.

Locomotive. A self-propelled, non-revenue rail vehicle designed to convert electrical or mechanical energy into tractive effort to haul railway cars.

Locomotive "A" Unit. The least number of wheel bases together with super-structures capable of independent propulsion and equipped with necessary appurtenances for use singly or as a lead unit in a locomotive combination.

Locomotive "B" Unit. The least number of wheel bases together with super-structures not capable of independent propulsion or capable of limited independent propulsion but not equipped with necessary appurtenances for use singly or as a lead unit in a locomotive combination.

Locomotive Crane. A power-operated crane, usually of the jib type, equipped to run on rails under its own power. The crane is erected on a special type of car body including propelling appraratus so that the power equipment which operates the lift can also be connected to the wheels. See Wrecking Crane.

Locomotive Unit. A single carbody with power and transmission equipment, but not necessarily with controls. Also called a "power unit," or, in the case of Diesel-Electric locomotives, a "Diesel Unit."

Logging Car. A special type of car for hauling or carrying logs usually consisting of two trucks and a skeleton frame, but sometimes provided with machinery and power for hauling by means of a cable.

Logging Truck. A truck used in logging cars. The member corresponding to the body bolster in other types of trucks is called a "bunk" and is so arranged that timber or logs may be chained in place on it.

Long Ton. A long or gross ton conists of 2,240 pounds.

Loop Station. A form of through station, in which the station track layout embraces a loop or part of a circle, trains being moved in one direction only, and in the process, being turned to run in the opposite direction.

Low Level (Flatcar). Referring to the height of a TOFC or auto rack flatcar deck above the top of the rail. Low level cars have a deck height of 31-1/2" as opposed to a 41-1/2" height for "standard level" cars.

Low Side Gondola. A gondola car with sides and ends no more than 36" high.

Lowry Process. An empty cell process for treating ties with creosote in which there is injected, without a preliminary vacuum, an amount of creosote in excess of the required final retention, this excess then being removed by a quick high vacuum.

LRC. Abbreviation for "light-rapid-comfortable."

LRV. Abbreviation for "light rail vehicle."

Lubricant. Any liquid or grease employed to coat a surface upon which another surface rotates or slides in order to reduce the friction.

Lubricating Oil System. The complete system on a Diesel electric locomotive for providing lubricating oil to the working parts of the engine.

Lug. Any projection on a component designed to afford a bearing surface or a point of securement to some other part. See Draft Lug.

Lunar White. One of the six standard colors used in railroad signaling.

L/V Ratio. The L/V ratio is defined as the ratio of the lateral force to the vertical force of a car or locomotive wheel on a rail. It is an important factor affecting the tendency of the wheel flange to climb the rail and/or the tendency to turn over under load, and is often a point of discussion in evaluating the cause of a train derailment.

M

Machine Frame. The support for the units of an interlocking machine.

Magnet. A body which possesses the property of attracting magnetic substances. Two common types in general use include electromagnets and permanent magnets.

Magnetic Circuit. The path through which magnetic flux passes.

Magnetic Coil. A conducting coil of insulated wire wound around the core of an electro-magnet.

Magnetic Field. A term applied to the space occupied by electric or magnetic lines of force.

Magnetic Field. A condition in the space surrounding a magnet, characterized by the existence of a detectable magnetic force.

Magnetic Flux. The number of lines of magnetic force that pass through a magnetic circuit.

Magnetic Particle Testing. A non-destructive test method for identifying cracks or discontinuities in castings or machined parts.

Magnetic Speed Indicator. A small magneto generator, driven from an axle, which shows on a dial in the cab the speed at any moment by the voltage developed at the terminals of the magneto.

Magneto. A small generator using permanent magnets for field poles.

Main Line. A term referring to the primary or most heavily used tracks of a railroad.

Main Reservoir. A cylindrical tank, carried on a locomotive or motor car, to hold a supply of compressed air. So called in distinction from the auxiliary and emergency reservoirs under each car.

Main Track. A track extending through yards and between stations, upon which trains are operated by timetable or train order, or both, or the use of which is governed by block signals. (Standard Code)

Male Center Plate. The car body center plate with its protruding bowl is sometimes called the "male center plate" as distinguished from its mating truck bolster center plate which is known as the "female center plate," the names being taken from the configuration of the two components.

Malleable Iron. Cast iron which has been heat treated to improve the toughness while retaining a good degree of ductility.

Manifest. A document giving the description of a single shipment or the contents of a car.

Manifold. A component of a piping system having multiple fittings allowing several lines to be connected to a common volume or supply, fed from or leading to a single line. Intake and exhaust manifolds on internal combustion engines are common examples.

Manipulation Chart. A statement in tabulated form showing the sequence in which levers or other devices must be operated.

Manual Block Signal System. A block signal system wherein the use of each block is governed by block signals controlled manually or by block-limit signals or both upon information by telephone or other means of communication.

Manual Interlocking. An interlocking that is operated manually as opposed to an automatic interlocking.

Manway. An opening in the dome of a tank car which permits access to the car's interior for such purposes as cleaning, inspecting and making repairs.

Marker. A lamp, reflector or flag mounted on a suitable bracket usually at the upper left and right corners of locomotives and caboose cars to indicate the front and rear ends of a train. Rear end markers always show red to the rear. Head end markers, where used, generally are white (to designate the train as an "extra") or green (to indicate that a second section of the same train is following behind).

Marker Light. A light which by its color or position, or both, qualifies the signal aspect.

Marline. A treated stranded cord.

Master Lever. A lever in an interlocking machine used to lock or unlock a group of levers.

Master Retarder. A retarder or retarders located between the apex of the hump and the master switch or switches in classification yard, and used specifically for car speed control.

Master Track Scale. A track scale especially designed for the calibration of railway test weight cars or for other special weighing where extreme accuracy is required.

Mate. A track structure having a fixed or immovable point and used on the opposite side of the track from a tongue switch, as its companion piece. A mate is termed "outside" or "inside" depending upon whether it is placed on the outside or inside of the curve; the "inside mate" being comparatively little used.

Mattress. A strong mat consisting of various materials, bound or woven together, used for the protection of the surface of the eroding banks or bottom of a river.

Maximum Gross Weight On Rails. For a single car, the maximum permissible weight of both car and lading permitted for operation in unrestricted interchange service. This figure is determined for any car by established Association of American Railroads Standards, and is related to the size of the axle journal in the trucks, and the diameter of the wheels under the car. For cars meeting A.A.R. design standards, the sum of the stenciled load limit and light weight will equal the maximum gross weight on rail allowed for that specific car.

Maximum Tractive Effort. As applied to locomotive equipment, the maximum force that may be exerted at the rims of the driving wheels. See Tractive Effort.

Measurement Ton. A term expressing 40 cubic feet.

Meat Rack (Refrigerator Car). The supports near the ceiling from which meat is suspended. Also called a "beef rail."

Mechanical Designation. An alphabetic code assigned by the Association of American Railroads to every freight car to designate its general design characteristics and its intended purpose. Mechanical designations are stenciled on every car on the same line and immediately to the right of the capacity stenciling.

Mechanical Refrigerator. A term applied to refrigerator cars equipped with a self-contained power plant and mechanical refrigeration equipment including a compressor, condenser, evaporator, and fans for distribution of cold air around the lading. The term is used to distinguish such cars from the older "ice" cars which relied on large blocks of ice placed in bunkers at the ends of the car to provide cooling.

Mechanical Trip (Trip Arm). A roadway element consisting in part of a movable arm that in operative position engages apparatus on the vehicle to effect an application of the brakes by the train-control system.

Medium Speed. A specific speed not to be exceeded when running under a particular signal indication as defined in the timetable of the railroad.

Memorandum Copy (Bill of Lading). One of the copies of a set of bill of lading forms; not the original copy. See Bill of Lading.

Messenger Wire. A wire used to support a cable. Also, in electrified territory, the energized transmission line that feeds the catenary, at various intervals.

Meter. One of the standard length measurements in the Metric system, equivalent to 39.368 inches in the English system.

Metric System. A decimal system for measuring length, capacity, surface and weight, using the meter as the unit of length, the liter as the unit of volume, and the gram as the unit of weight.

Metric Ton. A measure of weight equal to 2,240.6 pounds.

Metroliner. High speed multiple unit electric intercity passenger cars used on the electrified portion of the Northeast Corridor between New York City and Washington, D.C. Metroliner service has been extended to Boston using coaches similar to the original Metroliners hauled by a locomotive.

Middle Ordinate. On curves, the distance from the gage line of a rail to the center of the curve to the midpoint of a string drawn taut and held in contact with the gage line of a rail at the ends of the curve. It forms a convenient means of measuring curvature.

Middle Transom (Six-Wheel Trucks). The term applied to the two transoms nearest the center of the truck distinct from the two outside transoms.

Mileage Allowance. Free miles allowed by carriers to owners of private freight cars, based on various factors.

Mileage Basis. Method of charging for a car on an applicable rate per mile (instead of per diem) basis. Some private cars are on a per diem plus mileage rate.

Mileage Prorate. A division of revenue on interline shipments based on the percentage that each carrier's miles is to the total miles.

Mileage Rates. Rates based on mileage between points.

Mile Post. A post along a railroad right of way indicating the distance in miles to or from a given point.

Milling (of Rail). The cutting of the ends of rails with a milling hob to eliminate roughness and inaccuracies of sawing.

Minimum Carload Weight. The minimum weight, as provided for in a tariff, of an article that will be accepted for shipment, in order that it may be classed as a carload.

Minimum Charge. A fixed charge, below which no shipment will be accepted for transportation by the carrier.

Minimum Continuous Speed. The minimum speed at which a locomotive can operate continuously under heavy load condition without damaging the traction motors from high current (amperage). This speed is based on the maximum amperage the traction motor can accept without overheating.

Minimum Rates. Rates to be charged for moving traffic, as agreed upon by the carriers involved, below which the traffic will not be handled.

Minimum Reduction (Air Brake). A position on the 26-C Automatic Brake Valve quadrant used to obtain a very slight (6-8 lb.) brake pipe reduction and a very light brake application.

Mining Locomotive. A small locomotive operated by propane, compressed air or electricity for hauling cars in mines.

Misrouted Freight. Freight which through carriers' error is forwarded to correct destination via a route taking a higher rate than is applicable via route specified by shipper.

Mixed Carload. Two or more different commodities in the same car.

Mixed Carload Rate. The rate given a carload of different commodities in the same car.

Mixed Train. A railroad train consisting of both passenger and freight cars.

Modem. A contraction of the words modulator-demodulator; equipment that connects a data terminal to a communication line.

Modulus of Elasticity. The ratio, within the elastic limit of a material, of unit stress to corresponding unit strain or deformation.

Moisture Content. Amount of moisture in wood tie usually expressed as percentage of the dry weight of wood.

Motive Power. A term relating to the self-propelling equipment of a railroad, usually taken to mean locomotives.

Motor (Electric). A machine for converting electrical energy into mechanical energy in the form of rotary motion. It consists of a rotating armature turning in a magnetic field produced by an electric current. Motors for electric locomotives are built to operate on either alternation or direct current. Nearly all traction motors for diesel locomotives are series D.C. machines.

Motor Car. A car propelled by some form of motor located on the car itself. Preferably called "rail motor car." The common types of motor cars are: electric, which are equipped with electric motors and receive current from either a third rail or trolley wire; and those propelled by internal combustion engines which may have either electric or fluid drive.

Motor Cooling. The process of cooling traction motors usually by forced ventilation with air from motor driven blowers.

Motor Generator Set. An electric motor and an electric generator mechanically connected together. Their pincipal functions are for transforming electric currents of a given voltage to a higher or lower voltage, from direct to alternating current, from alternating to direct current or from one frequency to another on the locomotive. The set of machines is often referred to as an M-G Set.

Motor Truck. A powered truck under a rail motor car, M-U car or locomotive.

Movable Bridge. That section of a structure so designed that it may be displaced to permit passage of traffic.

Movable Bridge Coupler. A device for engaging and disengaging signal or interlocking connections between the shore and movable bridge span.

Movable Centerpoint. One of the two movable tapered rails of a movable point crossing or slip switch.

Movable Point Frog. A frog equipped with points which are movable in the same manner as the points on a switch.

Movable Point Crossing. A rail crossing at a flat angle where two movable points and a knuckle rail are used in place of each center frog.

M.P. The abbreviation for milepost, or motive power.

Mudguards (Tank Cars). Tank mounted metal shields which prevent mud from splashing off the car trucks onto the tank.

Mud-Sill (or Sub-Sill). A timber bedded in the ground to support a framed bent.

Muffler. A device attached to the exhaust manifold of an internal combustion engine to deaden noise.

Multi-Level Car. A term generally used to describe a long flatcar designed with an integral superstructure having one or more deck levels in addition to the main deck of the car, and fitted for the transportation of set up automobiles. See Automobile Rack Car, Bi-Level and Tri-Level Car.

Multiple Loading. Two or more carload shipments loaded in one car at the same origin for different destinations, or loaded in one car at different origins for complete unloading of a consignment at the same or different destinations.

Multiple Unit. A term referring to the practice of coupling two or more locomotives or electric passenger cars together with provision made to control the traction motors on all units from a single controller. Sometimes referred to as "MU."

Multiple-Wear Wheel. A steel railway wheel made with sufficient original rim thickness to permit turning full flange and tread contours at least twice during the life of the wheel.

Multi-Service Cars. Gondola or hopper cars adapted for transportation of bulk commodities and having a provision for optional discharge of same to center or to both sides of the track.

Multi-Unit Tank Car. A car consisting of a number of separate tanks or containers used for tansporting liquids in bulk.

N

Nailable Steel Floor. Flooring for box, gondola, and flatcars made of specially formed steel channel sections laid side by side generally across the car. The individual sections are kept a predetermined distance apart by spacer nubs embossed in the edges of the channels to enable nails to be driven into the grooves between adjacent sections. Blocking and bracing may thus be secured directly to the floor as with wooden flooring, but the advantages of steel are retained.

Name Plate. A small metal plate fastened to machines or other apparatus as a means of identifying the equipment, and after to provide information about its use.

Narrow Gage. A gage narrower than standard gage. A gage of 24 inches or less is commonly employed for industrial railways. Metric gage is commonly used in foreign countries.

National Railway Labor Conference. The U.S. railroad industry's bargaining arm in its negotiations with railway labor unions.

Needle Valve. An adjustable valve with a tapered point used in oil or air lines where fine regulation is required of the working fluid is required.

NFL Bearing. A factory lubricated journal roller bearing assembly made with superior seals and requiring no field lubrication during its normal service life. NFL bearings can be identified by the absence of a grease fitting in the end cap.

Net Ton-Miles. The number of tons of freight moved one mile.

Net Weight. The weight of an article without container, bag or covering, or, in case of carload freight, the weight of the entire contents of the car, but excluding the weight of the car itself.

Nipple A short piece of pipe with pipe threads turned on one or both ends and used for making connections in piping systems. See Air Brake Hose Nipple.

Node. When long trains are handled by helper locomotives, there is one point in the train where the pulling force exerted by the hauling locomotive is equalled by the pushing force exerted by the helping locomotive, resulting in a zero coupler force between the two cars at that point. This point of zero coupler force is called the node; it fluctuates constantly as the train negotiates undulating terrain, and the locomotive throttle settings are changed.

Nominal Capacity. The approximate load carrying capacity of a rail car to the nearest 1,000 pounds, based on car design, the size of the axle journals and the light weight of the car. The maximum nominal capacity that may be stenciled on a car is the next even 1,000 pounds equal to or below the stenciled load limit. Nominal capacity is stenciled on every freight car, and is designated CAPY.

Non-Piped Tank Car. A tank car not equipped with heating coils or insulation. Sometimes referred to as an "NP car."

Non-Pressure Head. The closure for the end of the brake cylinder not subjected to air pressure. The non-pressure head is tapered in the direction of piston travel, and has an opening for the hollow rod.

Normal Clear. A term used to express the normal indication of the signals in an automatic block system in which an indication to proceed is displayed except when the block is occupied.

Normalizing. A heat treatment process for iron based alloys resulting in controlled definite grain size, often done to relieve internal stresses or to impart the properties of strength and toughness.

Normally Aspirated (Internal Combustion Engine). An engine that uses air at atmospheric pressure for combustion.

Normal Speed. The maximum speed authorized by timetable.

Normal Stop. A term used to express the normal indication of the signals, in an automatic block system in which the indication to proceed is given only upon the approach of a train to an unoccupied block.

Nosing. A transverse, horizontal motion of a locomotive which exerts a lateral force on the supporting structure.

Nozzle. Any device containing one or more small openings through which a fluid is ejected under pressure.

O

Observation Car. A passenger train car equipped with an observation end with a portion of the car usually used as a buffet or lounge.

Obsolete Standard. A specification, procedure, practice, definition, design, product or device which was previously designated as Standard or Alternate Standard but which has been superseded, and which is restricted in interchange service subject to prescribed conditions. (A.A.R.)

Office Manual. One of two manuals that together form the A.A.R. Code of Interchange Rules governing the condition and repair of railway equipment used in interchange service. The Office Manual contains the pricing and billing information used for preparing bills for repair work done on foreign cars. See Interchange Rules and Field Manual.

Ohm. A unit of electric resistance. One ohm is equal to that resistance required to cause a one volt drop in potential when the current is one amp.

Ohmmeter. An instrument for measuring resistance in ohms.

Oil Cooler. A radiator or device made so that lubricating oil can be cooled after circulating through an internal combustion engine.

Oil Fount. A receptacle for housing the oil in a lamp.

Oil Pan. In internal combustion engines, a reservoir for lubricating oil, usually in the base of the engine.

Oil Ring. A ring located at the lower part of a piston to prevent an excess amount of oil from being drawn up onto the piston during the suction stroke.

One Spot. A car or locomotive repair shop designed so that the units of rail equipment to be repaired are moved progressively through the shop to various positions where specified work is done. Rip tracks designed with a single repair position equipped with modern jacking equipment, air, oxygen, and acetylene lines, lifting devices, and other time-saving equipment are sometimes referred to as "spot shops," or "one spots."

One-Wear Wheel. A steel railway wheel designed with a rim thickness such that full flange and tread contour can not be restored by turning. See Multiple Wear Wheel.

On-Line (Traffic). Traffic wholly on the line of a single carrier.

Open Air Distribution. Air distribution for refrigerator cars in which the tempered air is directed through the lading. This method is used primarily for fresh produce.

Open-Book Account. A form of credit based on an informal but valid contract between the carrier and shipper or consignee; with the shipper, evidenced by the prepaid bill of lading, and with the consignee, by a signed delivery receipt of the collect freight bill.

Open Circuit. An incomplete electric circuit.

Open Station. A station where an agent is located and to which freight may be shipped charges collect.

Open-Top Car. Any of a group of cars with or without sides and ends, and with no roof, all being intended for transportation of commodities not requiring protection from the weather, such as steel products, coal or rough forest products. Flat, gondola and hopper cars are all classed as open-top cars.

Open-Top Loading Rules. A set of standard rules and regulations issued by the Association of American Railroads governing the methods used for loading and securing commodities on open-top cars.

Operating Expenses. The principal debit account recording the expense of operating, maintaining and administering the transportation company's property and performing the various services for which operating revenues are received.

Operating Platform An arrangement around the manway on tank cars, built to provide a flat surface and safety railing for workers involved in loading and/or unloading operations on top of the tank.

Operating Ratio. The ratio of operating costs to gross revenue.

Operating Revenues. The principal credit account recording the income derived by a transportation company directly or indirectly from the service of transporting passengers, freight, mail, express and other services incidental to the general business of transportation.

Operating Rules. The book of rules governing the conduct of transportation on a particular railroad, and defining signal indications, speeds and other specific operating requirements.

Opposed-Piston Engine. A diesel engine, with two pistons per cylinder, traveling away from each other during the power stroke and toward each other during the compression stroke. There are two crankshafts, connected through a bevel-geared shaft at right angles to the crankshafts.

Opposing Signals. Signals which govern movements in opposite directions on the same track.

Opposing Train. A train moving toward and in the opposite direction from another train on the same track.

Ore Car. An open top gondola or hopper car designed specifically to carry iron or some other metallic ore. Because of the high density of most ores, cars for this service are built with relatively low cubic capacities, and some are equipped with empty and load brake equipment.

Orifice. A calibrated opening through which a fluid flows.

Origin (of Traffic). The location where a shipment begins.

Original Record of Repairs. The written record of repairs made to a foreign railroad car on a railroad rip track, and prepared at the time the repairs are performed. The original record of repairs becomes the basis for billing the car owner for repairs according to standards prescribed in the Interchange Rules.

O.S.&D. Room. A room in larger freight stations providing for the handling of unclaimed, short weight or damaged items.

Outboard Bearing. A bearing outside the engine proper carrying an extension of the crankshaft.

Outfit (or Camp Car). Car equipped with facilities for feeding and housing construction and maintenance employees.

Outlet Valve. The valve on a tank car by means of which the lading is discharged from the tank.

Outrigger. Heavy beams, with jack screws at the ends, which are put out on each side of a steam shovel or a locomotive crane at the forward bolster and supported on blocking. They prevent the carbody from overturning due to the reaction of the load on the boom.

Overcharge (Air Brake). A condition where the brake equipment on the train has been charged to a pressure greater than the pressure that can be normally supplied from the controlling locomotive. See Taper.

Overhang. That portion of the body of a railway car between the body bolster and the end sill. Long cars with large overhangs require special wide mouth striker openings to accommodate the lateral swing of the long shank couplers that must be used.

Overhead Contact Shoe. A metal bar for collecting current from an overhead conductor along which it slides. It is held in place by a pantograph or bow.

Overhead Loading. A method of loading highway trailers or containers on intermodal cars by the use of an overhead (usually a gantry type) crane. See Circus Loading and Side Loading.

Overhead Traffic. Freight traffic moving over a line which was received from a connecting line and will be delivered to a connecting line. Also known as "Bridge Traffic." See Intermediate Carrier.

Overlap. The distance the control of one signal extends into the territory which another signal, or signals, governs.

Overload. A load greater than that which a device is designed to carry.

Over, Short and Damage Report. A report submitted by a freight agent showing discrepancies in billing received and freight on hand.

Overspeed Control. A safety device that will cause a penalty brake application to occur when the speed of a locomotive exceeds that of the overspeed setting.

Overspeed Protection. A device to automatically shut down an engine on a locomotive if the engine speed exceeds a predetermined value.

Overthrow. The excess stroke of a switch operation rod.

Ownership Plate. A casting or stencil giving the name of the bank or trust company that furnished the funds to build the equipment and in whom ownership of the equipment resides.

P

Packing. A general term denoting the various substances and devices used to prevent leakage of fluids or gases through openings which cannot be closed by ordinary contact of the parts concerned. This definition should not be confused with journal box packing which really functions as a form of lubricator.

Packing Block. A small member, usually wood, used to secure the parts of a composite member in their proper relative positions.

Packing Cup. A specially designed packing component that fits on the base of the piston of the AB brake cylinder and presses against the cylinder walls to seal against air leakage during brake applications.

Panel. A board or support for electric switches and other apparatus.

Pantograph. A device for collecting current from an overhead conductor (catenary) and consisting of a jointed frame operated by springs or compressed air, and having a suitable collector at the top.

Parallel (Electric Circuit). A method of connecting two or more pieces of electrical apparatus of a common circuit so that the positive poles of each are connected to a common positive conductor and the negative poles are connected to a common negative conductor. See Series.

Parlor Car. A passenger train car for day travel, having revolving or movable seats, smoking compartments, and other ammenities not found in coaches. An extra fare is generally charged for travel.

Passenger Mile. A term denoting the transportation of one passenger for a distance of one mile.

Passenger Tariff. A schedule containing passenger rates (fares), excess baggage charges, routing, rules and privileges.

Passing Report. A listing of the cars received or delivered in interchange or moving between yards; usually required by Traffic Department as basis for disseminating car movement information to shippers and consignees, and for auditor's office, particularly on overhead or "bridge" traffic.

Passing Track. A track auxiliary to the main track for meeting of passing trains. Same as "siding."

Pawl. A specially shaped pivoting steel piece arranged to fall into notches or teeth of a wheel as it rotates in one direction, thus restraining rotation of the wheel in the opposite direction. See Brake Pawl.

Pedestal (Roller Bearing). That portion of a roller bearing truck side frame that takes the vertical load from the axle journals through the roller bearing adapters, and serves to retain the ends of the axle in the proper longitudinal relationalship to the truck and to the rails.

Pedestal Spring. A spring which rests on a journal box between the jaws of a pedestal.

Pedestal Stay Rod. A transverse rod connecting the pedestal tie bars on each side of a truck to prevent them from spreading.

Pedestal Tie Bar. A bar extending across the mouth of a pedestal jaw underneath a journal box and bolted to the jaws of the pedestal. Also a bar sometimes called "pedestal strap," connecting two or more pedestals on the same side of a truck or car.

Pedestal Trucks. Railway trucks designed with side frames having pedestals at each end to retain the journal bearings, as distinguished from side frames with journal boxes cast integral for use with plain bearing axles.

Penalty Application. An automatic application of air brakes caused by a locomotive overspeed or by the release of the safety control foot pedal with the locomotive brakes released.

Penetration. The consistency of a bituminous material expressed as the distance that a standard needle vertically penetrates a sample of the material under known conditions of loading, time and temperature.

Penetration (Wood Treatment). The depth to which preservative enters ties through both lateral and end surfaces.

Per Diem. The amount or rate paid by one carrier to another or to a private car owner for each calendar day (or each hour) it uses a car belonging to the other.

Performance Control System. A system which automatically controls the horsepower output of a locomotive during low speed operation to provide maximum tractive effort within the adhesion capabilities of the locomotive. This system also allows compatible operation with lower horsepower locomotives.

Permanent Magnet. A material retaining its magnetic properties without the use of any external energy.

Permanent Set. The strain or deformation remaining in a body after being stressed beyond the elastic limit.

Permeability. A term used to express the ability of a substance, such as iron or steel, to support magnatism.

Permissive Block. A block in manual or controlled manual territory, which may permit a train, other than a passenger train, to follow a train, other than a passenger train, in the block, in accordance with prescribed rules.

Phantom Signal Aspect. A light signal display, different from the aspect intended, caused by a light from an external source being reflected by the optical system of the signal.

Photo-Electric Cell. A device which is sensitive to light and which will control electrical circuits in response to changes in light intensity or color.

Pick. A pointed steel tool used to deliver blows to loosen or remove matter.

Pickup. A term descriptive of a car or cars added to a train enroute between dispatching and receiving yards; or added at dispatching yard to train operating over two or more divisions on a continuous wheel report.

Piggyback. A term referring to the practice of transporting highway trailers on railroad flatcars. See TOFC.

Piggyback Cars. Flatcars designed and equipped for the transportation of highway vehicles or containers.

Pike Pole. A long handled pole with a sharp point and hook to handle timber logs, or ties.

Pile. A member usually driven or jetted into the ground and deriving its support from the underlying strata, and by the friction of the ground on its surface. The usual functions of a pile are: to carry a superimposed load; to compact the surrounding ground; to form a wall to exclude water and soft material, or to resist the lateral pressure of adjacent ground.

Pile Driver. A machine for driving piles.

Pile Hammer. A weight used to drive piles. It may be designated as a steam hammer, diesel hammer or drop hammer, depending on the source of energy.

Pilot. A qualified employee assigned to a train or other on-track equipment when the engineer, conductor or driver is not qualified on the physical characteristics or rules of the portion of the railroad over which movement is to be made.

Pinion. The smaller of two gears in a gear chain.

Pipe Bracket. That portion of an air brake control valve or other air brake apparatus which is secured to the car underframe, and to which pipe connections are made. The ABD pipe bracket is designed with two machined surfaces which exactly match the surfaces of the emergency and service portions of the equipment, so that these operating portions may be removed for periodic cleaning without disturbing the pipe connections to the valve.

Pipe Carrier. A device to guide and support signal pipe across tracks.

Pipe Clamp. A clamp for holding air or steam pipes in place, consisting of a fixed piece welded to the car underframe and a mating piece driven tight with a hammer when the pipe is in place.

Pipe Coupling. A device by which two lengths of pipe may be connected.

Piped Rail. A rail defect in the form of a vertical split, usually in the web, due to failure of the side of the shrinkage cavity in the ingot to unite in rolling.

Pipe Guide. An arrangement usually made of a bar of iron which is securely fastened in place for the purpose of guiding the movements of a pipe which is connected to some part of an interlocking.

Pipe Line. A length of pipe with appropriate fittings and valves for conducting a fluid.

Pipe Offset. A casting in the form of a reverse curve designed for the continuation of a line of pipe around some obstacle in a line parallel to its beginning.

Pipe Union. A device by which two lengths of pipe may be connected without turning the pipe.

Piston. A disc or clylinder made to fit closely to the inside diameter of another cylinder, and having packing or rings to seal against leakage past its outer edges. When pressure is exerted on the face of the piston by a gas or other fluid, it moves within the cylinder, thus imparting linear motion to a piston rod attached to the center of the piston on the non-pressure side, and extending outside the cylinder.

Piston Pin. A pin which rests in two bored holes in the piston and passes through the eye of the connecting rod, to join the two together flexibly. Also known as "wrist pin."

Piston Ring. A metal ring that snaps into a groove around the circumference of a piston to prevent leakage of the working fluid between the piston and the walls of the cylinder.

Piston Rod. A rod secured at one end to a piston, and extending outside the cylinder where it is connected to some mechanism to be operated by the compressed fluid within the cylinder. The piston rod in an air brake system on a railway car is called the hollow rod, so named because it is a hollow tube into which the push rod fits.

Piston Travel. The amount of linear movement of the air brake hollow rod or piston rod when forced outward by movement of the piston in the brake cylinder and limited by the brake shoes being forced against the wheel. Good brake efficiency depends on the slack in the brake system being maintained at a point where piston travel will not exceed a specified value, depending on foundation rigging design.

Pitting. Localized corrosion.

Pivot Pin. Another name for the knuckle pin in a coupler.

Placard Card Holder. A steel frame designed to hold and display cards describing the nature of dangerous commodities being transported in a railway tank car.

Plain Bearing. As distinguished from a journal roller bearing; a journal bearing arrangement whereby a brass or bronze bearing is held in place against a polished axle journal, and lubricated by free oil in a journal box fed to the bearing by a lubricating device.

Plate. The term when used alone, means any flat piece of steel or other material having significant length, width and thickness, and suitable for construction purposes. A sheet is the same as a plate only thinner. There are many special car components, some flat and some formed, that carry the name "plate" as part of their identification; such as side plate, deck plate or end plate. See Wheel Plate.

Plate, Center. See Center Plate.

Plate Cutting. The wearing away of the tie under the base of the rail or tie plate.

Plate, Name. A plate affixed to a device giving the manufacturer's name and other information.

Plate, Riser. A plate attached to a gage or tie plate used to support and raise a switch point above the base of rail and maintain minimum gage.

Plate, Tie. A plate interposed between a rail or other track structure and a tie. (A.R.E.A.)

Platform. In the general sense, any raised or supported flat surface designed to serve some specific purpose. Usually an additional explanatory term is used with the word such as "end platform" or "brake platform" to more clearly identify the specific use.

Platform Casting (Car Construction). A steel casting which forms the frame of the platform and the underframe of the car back, to and including the body bolster, at which point it is secured to the structural steel underframe members.

Platform Steps (Passenger Cars). The stairs at the corner of a car which afford the means of entering and exiting.

Platform Trap Door. A door which covers the space over the steps, thus extending the platform out to the side of the car.

Plug. In electrical work, the fixture attached to the end of a wire or cable to provide a means for connecting the cable to some device or to another cable. Male plugs have projecting prongs, while female plugs have slots or open clips to receive the prongs, and are sometimes called "receptacles." In pipe work, a plug is a small cylinder with external threads that can be screwed into the end of a pipe to seal the opening.

Plug Coupler. A movable couple designed to engage and connect to a coupler socket.

Plug Door. A type of side door used on insulated box and refrigerator cars that fits flush with the interior car side when closed. Plug doors provide a better seal and are, therefore, more desirable than the common sliding door for insulated car applications.

Plunger. The piston in a high pressure pump such a fuel injector.

Pneumatic Bulkhead. A load securement device used in some boxcars, consisting of heavy inflatable air bags, sandwiched between two vertical bulkheads that exert longitudinal pressure against the lading when the air bags are pressurized. Lading is restrained from both lateral and longitudinal movement in transit by the force exerted by the bulkheads reacting at the ends of the car.

Pneumatic Foot Valve. The foot operated air valve in a locomotive safety system sometimes known as the "deadman" valve. The valve must be continously depressed while operating the locomotive. If the engineman releases the foot pedal, a warning whistle sounds, followed by a penalty brake application.

Pocket. A term sometimes used to describe the space between the webs of a draft sill that contains the draft gear or end-of-car-cushion unit. See Draft Gear Pocket.

Point Lug. A lug bolted to the web of a switch point rail, to which the switch circuit controller rod is attached.

Pool Cars. Car operating pursuant to a car pooling agreement among and between railroads. See Car Pooling.

Pooled Shipments. Less-than-carload shipments loaded into one car and billed as solid or mixed carload to take advantage of carload rate or carload service.

Pooling Agreement. The agreement between railroads covering the details of operation of a pool of equipment to which each carrier contributes and from which, each derives a share of revenue. See Car Pooling.

Port. An opening in a valve or cylinder for the passage of a fluid.

Position Light Signal. A fixed signal in which the indications are given by the position of two or more lights.

Post. Any vertical member of a car body super structure.

Pot Signal. A small revolving fixed signal used as a substitute for a dwarf signal.

Pouch Check. An inspection made by the A.A.R. Car Service Division at certain points, showing the transit of all freight in selected cars being worked at a station or transfer on the date of the check to determine transit time of freight, generally made for the purpose of locating a delay.

Pour Point. The lowest temperature at which locomotive lubricating oil will barely flow measured under standard test conditions.

Power. The rate of doing work.

Power Plant. Any independent system of machines used to generate electricity from some other form of energy, such as gasoline, fuel oil, coal, or flowing water. As applied to mechanical refrigeration systems on rail cars, the power plant consists of a diesel or gasoline engine coupled to a generator, with all necessary controls.

Pressure. A unit force generally measured in terms of pounds per square inch (or kilograms per square centimeter) created by the action of a compressed gas or fluid in a confined space.

Pressure Head. On a railway car brake cylinder, the closure over the end of the brake cylinder into which air pressure is admitted when the brakes are applied.

Pressure Maintaining Feature. A feature of the air brake system on locomotives that serves to overcome normal train line leakage, and allows any desired brake pipe pressure to be maintained for long periods of time during service applications of the train air brake.

Pressure Regulator. Any device in a system to regulate the pressure of a working fluid in the system.

Private Car. Passenger equipment—a business car assigned to specific official of a railroad for his personal use in conducting company business and making inspections. Freight equipment—any car operated in interchange, and owned by a shipper or some independent car leasing firm, as distinguished from a car owned by a railroad. A private freight car may usually be distinguished from a railroad owned car by the letter "X" used as the last letter in the car reporting marks.

Private Car Line. A private concern owning its own rolling equipment or leasing cars to or from railroads and operating them as private cars.

Private Siding (Track). A sidetrack, owned or leased by an industry, on which cars are placed for loading or unloading.

Profile. A line representing the ground surface or an established grade line, or both, in relation to the horizontal.

Propane. A petroleum product made primarily from natural gas and generally used as a fuel at remote locations not served by pipelines. It is usually shipped as a compressed liquid in heavy metal containers or in bulk in 33,000 gallon pressure tank cars.

Proportional Rate. A rate applying as a proportion on a part of the route of a shipment between one station and another, but moving between the two stations, either originating beyond the first or destined beyond the second. For example; A rate from Syracuse, N.Y., to St. Joseph, Mo., is made up of the rate to the Mississippi River from the point of origin plus the rate (proportional) to St. Joseph. This porportional rate is less than if the shipment had originated at a Mississippi River point.

Propulsion Bond. A low-resistance conductor providing a path for the return propulsion current at non-insulated joints.

Prorating Territory. Indicative of a territory to which are published through rates that divide on percentages between carriers involved.

Protective Controls. Controls which automatically function to protect the locomotive, its engine or the electrical equipment under abnormal conditions resulting from failures of various parts of the equipment to function correctly.

Protective Services. Specific services rendered enroute, such as refrigeration, icing, salting, heating etc., for which charges and allowances are made by tariff authority.

Pulley. A wheel generally with a grooved surface around the circumference, adapted to receive a cord, belt or chain which runs over it. Pulleys are used to transmit power, to change the direction of motion or, in a block and tackle arrangement, to enable the multiplication of force at the expense of speed. Another term often used for pulley is "sheave wheel."

Pull Iron. A roping staple.

Pump Governor. A device for regulating the pressure of fluid delivered by a pump by controlling the power delivered to the pump.

Pump Stage. A term used in connection with centrifugal pumps to indicate the number of impellers, a single stage pump having one impeller, a two stage pump two impellers, etc.

Purlin or Purline. A longitudinal roof frame member extending over the carlines, to which the roof sheets are fastened.

Push Car. A four-wheeled work car, designed to be pushed by hand; sometimes used as a trailer with a motor car, and supplied to maintenance employees for transporting materials too heavy to be carried on a hand car. See Hand Car.

Push Pole Pocket. A semi-spherical cavity at the lower corners of older freight cars and locomotives (often a design feature of the corner casting) to enable a locomotive to push a car from a parallel track by use of a long pole inserted in the cavity. Safety considerations have made this practice obsolete, and newer cars are not equipped with push-pole pockets.

Push Rod. The rod which transmits force from the piston rod of a brake cylinder (the hollow rod) to the foundation brake gear on the car. The push rod fits loosely into the cylinder hollow rod and has a formed jaw on its outer end to enable a pin connection to be made to the cylinder lever. As brake cylinder pressure builds up, the collar of the hollow rod pushes against the back of the jaw on the push rod and forces it outward to apply the car brakes through the foundation rigging. Since the push rod is free to move within the hollow rod, a manual brake application can be made with the hand brake without the necessity of overcoming the frictional resistance of the brake cylinder piston.

Q

Quick Service. A term used to describe the initial stage of an air brake application on a freight car. During quick service, certain parts in the service portion of the control valve operate to create a local reduction in brake pipe pressure on each car to produce a rapid and positive brake application simulataneously throughout the train. This phase of brake application is sometimes referred to as "preliminary quick service."

R

"R" Side. The side of a rail car on the right of the observer when facing the "B" end of the car.

Rack. In machinery, a rectilinear sliding piece, with teeth cut on its edge for working with a gear wheel. In car construction, a supplementary structure on the basic car body to facilitate the loading of specialized cargo.

Radius of Curvature. A measure of the severity of a curve in a track structure based on the length of the radius of a circle that would be formed if the curve were continued. Freight cars designed to Association of American Railroads standards must negotiate curves of stated minimum radii without wheel or truck interference with brake rigging or structural underframe members.

Rail. As used in car construction, any horizontal member of a car superstructure. The term is usually used in combination with some additional identifying word such as "belt rail" or "hand rail." As used in track, a rolled steel shape, commonly a T-section, designed to be laid end to end in two parallel lines on cross ties or other suitable supports to form a track for railway rolling stock.

Rail Anchor. A device attached to the base of a rail bearing against a crosstie to prevent the rail from moving longitudinally under traffic.

Rail Bond. A short metal cable attached to adjacent rails at the joints to insure proper electrical continuity across the joint.

Rail Brace. A bracing device used at switches, movable point frogs, etc., in combination with switch, tie or gage plates for holding the rail in place.

Rail Clip. A device bolted or clamped to a rail, for supporting and guiding a detector bar.

Rail Creep. Longitudinal sliding of rails in track under traffic or because of temperature changes.

Rail Diesel Car. A self-propelled passenger car used in commuter or branch line service. RDC's have their own power plant, and can be operated in MU service with serveral cars controlled from the lead car.

Rail Joint. A fastening designed to unite the abutting ends of contiguous rails.

Rail Lubricator. A device designed to apply grease to the gage side of the rail head at the beginning of a curve. In order to minimize wear of the rail and wheel flange or to eliminate noise.

Railroad Retirement Act. An Act of Congress, August 29, 1935, for the purpose of establishing a retirement system for employees subject tothe Interstate Commerce Act.

Railroad Retirement Board. A board consisting of three members appointed by the President, by and with the consent of the Senate, to administer the Railroad Retirement Act.

Railroad Tie. The transverse member of the track structure to which the rails are spiked or otherwise fastened to provide proper gage and to cushion, distribute, and transmit the stresses of traffic through the ballast to the roadbed.

Rail Saw. A power machine, provided with a saw of either tooth or friction type, used to cut steel rails.

Rail Section. The shape of the end of a rail cut at right angles to its length. The rail mills identify the different shapes and types of rails by code numbers, as for example, 131-28 for the 131 RE rail section.

Rail Web. See Web.

Railway Labor Act. An Act of Congress, May 20, 1926, Amended June 21, 1934, providing for the disposition of disputes between carrier and employees. The 1934 Amendment created the National Railroad Adjustment Board and National Mediation Board.

Railway Service Car. A general term applied to cars used for maintenance of way, construction, wreck service etc. Including such cars as "Ballast", "Instructional", "Scoop", "Snow Plows", and "Wrecking Cars."

Railway System. The entire trackage, equipment and facilities of a line-haul railroad, inclusive of main tracks, side tracks, branch lines, yards and terminals.

Raised-Wheel Seat Axle. See Axle.

Rapid Transit. A term referring to urban high speed rail systems for moving people, including subways, elevated lines, and surface lines.

Ratchet. A device having serrated teeth similar to sawteeth, that works in conjunction with a pawl to prevent motion in one direction while allowing motion in the opposite direction.

Rate. The movement and handling of goods or persons, the determining factor used in arriving at the charge or fare for services rendered.

Rate Bureau. The tariff publication agency for all carriers within a certain freight classification territory.

Rate of Return. The ratio of net operating income (also called "net railway operating income" in railway accounting) to the value of the property in common carrier use, including allowance for working capital.

Rate Prorate. A division of revenue on interline shipments on the percentage basis which each carrier's local rate to or from the interchange point is to the total combination rate from origin to destination. See Divisions of Revenue.

Rate Schedule. See Tariff.

Rate Structure. The foundation upon which a series of related rates are based. See Rate.

Rear (of a Signal). The side of the signal from which the indication is received, not the back of the signal.

Receiver (Train Control). A device on a locomotive, so placed that it is in position to be influenced inductively or actuated by an automatic train stop, train control, or cab signal roadway element. (I.C.C.)

Receiving Yard. A rail yard generally used for receiving trains over the road movements.

Receptacle. In electrical systems, a device for receiving a plug. Together the plug and receptacle allow for rapid and positive positive connection of cables having multiple conductors.

Reciprocal Switching. A mutual interchange of inbound and outbound carload freight which is switched to or from a siding of another carrier under a regular switching charge. The charge is usually absorbed by the carrier receiving the line haul.

Recommended Practice. A specification, design, product or device which is accepted by the A.A.R. for use on rolling stock. A recommended practice shall not substitute for a Standard or Alternate Standard. (A.A.R.)

Reconsignment. Changes in consignee or destination before or after arrival of shipment at original destination.

Rectifier. A device which converts alternating current into direct current by virtue of a characteristic permitting appreciable flow of current in one direction only. (I.E.E.E.)

Recupping. Reforming the head of a rivet after it has been driven.

Red Lead. An oxide made from metallic lead and used as a preservative coating on steel. It is frequently painted on the surfaces where two pieces of metal are jointed as in riveting.

Reduced Speed. Proceed prepared to stop short of train or obstruction. (Standard Code)

Reducing Valve. A valve for air or steam that receives the fluid at a certain pressure and delivers it at a predetermined lower pressure.

Reduction (Air Brake). A decrease in brake pipe pressure at a rate and of an amount sufficient to cause a train brake application to be initiated or increased.

Reefer. A common slang term for a "Refrigerator Car."

Refrigerator Car. A closed car built with insulation in the floor, sides, ends, roof, and doors, and some form of refrigeration equipment designed for handling commodities requiring cooling during transit. Some refrigerator cars are also equipped with heaters for protection of perishable commodities during sub-freezing weather.

Regenerative Braking. The retardation system on electric cars or locomotives which can return power developed by traction motors acting as generators to the third rail or trolley for use by other units.

Region. The part of the railroad under the jurisdiction of the General Superintendent--Operations.

Regular Train. A train represented on the timetable.

Reinforcement. A supplementary part of a structure that strengthens the main carrying members.

Reinforcing Rail. A bent rail placed with its head along the outside of and close to the head of a knuckle rail to strengthen it and to act as an easer rail; or a piece of rail similarly applied to a movable center point.

Relay. A device that is operative by a variation in the conditions of one electric circuit to affect the operation of other devices in the same or another electric circuit.

Relay Rails. Rails taken up from tracks where formerly used, which are suitable for relaying in other tracks.

Relay, Retained Neutral Polarized. A polarized relay, the neutral armature of which is retained in the energized position for a predetermined interval of open circuit during the reversal of current in the control coils.

Relay, Track. A relay receiving all or part of its operating energy through conductors of which the track rails are an essential part.

Release Rod. A small rod situated at the side sill for the purpose of operating the air brake release valve.

Release Spring. A helical spring situated in the brake cylinder so as to exert an inward force on the piston and thereby assist in moving the piston to the released position as cylinder pressure is exhausted to atmosphere.

Release Valve. A valve permitting auxiliary reservoir air pressure to be released when the locomotive is detached or when the apparatus is out of order, so as to release or "bleed" the brakes.

Relief Track. An extended siding long enough to allow a train of inferior class to continue running while the superior train occupies the main track.

Relief Valve. A valve, usually held closed by a spring and which is forced open when pressure in the vessel to which it is attached rises above a predetermined value. Often called a safety valve.

Remote Control. A term denoting the control of any apparatus from a location apart from the location of the apparatus.

Repeater. A device conveying information about the condition of a piece of operating machinery by repeating instrument readings (pressures, temperatures etc.) as they exist at the machine, and displaying the same reading at some other location.

Reporting Marks. The alphabetical initials such as or that are stencilled on the sides and ends of every freight car to identify the railroad or private car line that owns the car. Reporting marks are assigned by the Association of American Railroads, and in conjunction with the car number, serve to uniquely identify every car in the interchange fleet.

Rerailer. A portable device designed so that when placed next to the rail, a derailed car or locomotive wheel, when rolled over it, will be guided back onto the rail.

Reservoir. In a fluid system, a tank or other vessel used to contain a supply of the working fluid to make the system function properly. In a car air brake system, the large two-compartment tank that contains compressed air to operate the brake cylinder when the brakes are applied. See Auxiliary Reservoir and Emergency Reservoir.

Resistance. In general, resistance denotes opposition to movement or flow. In mechanical systems, any force that opposes motion such as friction or action of a spring could be termed as resistance. In electrical circuits, resistance is opposition to the flow of current, and is measured in units called Ohms.

Restoring Feature. An arrangement on a power-operated switch movement by means of which power is applied to restore the switch movement to full normal or to full reverse position, before the driving bar creeps sufficiently to unlock the switch, with control lever in normal or reverse position. (I.C.C.)

Restricted Speed. A speed governed by timetable instructions and related to various signal indications as defined in the operating rules of a particular railroad.

Retainer. The usual term for the pressure retaining valve on freight cars. This manually operated valve can be set to retain a predetermined pressure in the brake cylinder even after the brakes are released, so that the brakes can remain applied on heavy grades while the brake pipe and auxiliary reservoir pressures are restored after a brake application.

Retarder. A braking device, usually power-operated, built into a railway track to reduce the speed of cars by means of brake-shoes which, when set in braking position, press against the sides of the lower portions of the wheels. (A.R.E.A.)

Retarder, Intermediate. A retarder which is located between master or hump retarder and group retarder, generally employed only at larger yards.

Revenue Ton-Mile. The movement of a ton of 2,000 pounds of revenue freight a distance of one mile.

Reverse Curve. Curves composed of two simple curves which join at a common tangent point or by a short tangent track or a reverse easement curve, and seen in opposite direction.

Reverser. The handle on a locomotive control stand that selects the direction in which the locomotive will move by reversing the traction motor field connections.

Rheostat. A device used to vary the resistance in an electric circuit as a means of controlling the current flowing in the circuit.

Rider Track. A track in a hump yard on which some type of wheeled car is operated for returning car riders to the summit of the hump .

Ridge Cap. A flanged metal strip to cover the ridge joint on a metal car roof.

Right of Way. The strip of land on which a railroad truck is built. The term generally refers to intercity main line tracks, but can also apply to branch lines and sidings.

Rigid Wheel Base. The horizontal distance between the centers of the first and last axles of a locomotive truck.

Rim. On a railway car wheel, that portion around the outer circumference that forms the edge of the tread. The thickness of the rim is a measure of the amount of wear remaining in the wheel, and when this dimension reaches a given limit (as measured with the A.A.R. steel wheel gage), the wheel must be scrapped.

Ring Grooves (Internal Combustion Engine). Grooves cut in the piston barrel to hold the piston rings.

Rip Track. A small car repair facility, often simply a single track in a classification yard or terminal. In larger yards, the rip track may be quite extensive with several tracks and shop buildings. Larger car repair facilities are generally known as "car shops". The name "rip track" is derived from the initials RIP which stand for "repair, inspect and paint."

Riprap. Large pieces of rock or other hard material used to provide a foundation on soft ground.

Riser. In car construction, the transverse load bearing members applied to the deck of a flatcar, the purpose of which is to support the lading a specified distance above the car floor to facilitate loading and unloading operations using mechanized equipment. A riser is also the vertical panel between the treads in a stairway.

Riser Boards. Wooden or steel longitudinal members applied to the deck of a TOFC car adjacent to and on either side of the trailer hitch, the purpose of which is to provide the necessary clearance between the hitch and the undercarriage of the vehicles passing over it.

Rivet. A short cylindrical steel rod with a semi-spherical upset head used to fasten parts of a steel structure together. Rivets generally have one head formed prior to positioning, and the other is formed after the joint is assembled, either with hydraulic pressure in a ram (cold riveting), or with air operated riveting guns and a bucking tool (hot riveting).

Roadbed. The foundation on which the rails and ties of a railroad are placed.

Roadway Element. That portion of the roadway apparatus of automatic train stop, train control or cab signal system, such as electric circuit, inductor, magnet, ramp or trip arm to which the locomotive apparatus of such system is directly responsive. (I.C.C.)

Rock and Roll. A slang term for the excessive lateral rocking of cars, usually at low speeds and associated with jointed rail. The speed range which this cyclic phenomenon occurs is determined by such factors as the wheel base, height of the center of gravity of each individual car, and the spring dampening associated with each vehicle's suspension system.

Rocker Arm. A lever, usually mounted on a shaft on the cylinder head, which has one end resting on the valve stem top and the outer end resting on a push rod whose motion lifts the rocker arm which in turn pushes the valve open.

Rod, Operating. In general, any rod by means of which motion is transmitted to an apparatus.

Rodman. A person in a surveying crew who holds the rod.

Rollability. A term generally applied in classification yards pertaining to the characteristics of individual cars and their ability to roll.

Roller Bearing. The general term applied to any group of journal bearings that employ hardened steel rollers to reduce rotational friction. Roller bearings are sealed assemblies that are mechanically pressed onto an axle, and transfer the wheel loads to the truck side frames through a device known as a roller bearing adapter that fits between the bearing outer ring and the side frame pedestal.

Roller Bearing Adapter. A casting that fits between a freight car roller bearing and the truck side frame to transfer the load from the side frame to the bearing.

Roller Bearing Key. A retainer for securing a roller bearing assembly in its proper position in the side frame.

Roller Side Bearing. A side bearing fitted with rollers to reduce the friction in curving. See Side Bearings.

Rolling Stock. A general term used when referring collectively to a large group of railway cars.

Roof Hand Hold. A bar bent to a required shape and fastened to the roof to be grasped when ascending the ladder at the end of the car. Also called "roof grab iron."

Roof Ridge. On a pitched roof, the intersection of the two plain surfaces along the peak, generally at the longitudinal center line of the car.

Roof Sheet. The relatively thin steel sheet that is used in fabricating roof sections for freight cars. Roof sheets are often galvanized for protection against rust.

Rotary Coupler. A type of freight car coupler used generally on high side gondola cars for coal service with a design feature in the shank that allows the coupler to rotate axially with respect to the draft sill. This feature enables cars to remain coupled while passing through rotary car dumpers, and thus enhances unit train operation by eliminating the need to break up trains for unloading.

Rotary Dump Car. A high side gondola or hopper car equipped with a rotary coupler on one end to enable unloading by means of a rotaty car dumper.

Rotary Operated Coupler. A freight car coupler that is equipped with a bottom operated lock lift mechanism as opposed to the top operated type. The mechanism, located under the coupler head, is termed the rotary operating mechanism because it rotates through an arc when actuated by movement of the uncoupling rod. Not to be confused with rotary coupler.

Rotor. The rotating member of motors, generators or motor type relays.

Roundel. In signalling, a glass or similar product, usually circular in shape, used in lens or reflector assemblies for producing color or for mechanical protection of critical parts, or for spreading or deflecting the projected light beam into a pattern, dependent upon the design. It may be clear or colored as required.

Roundel Clip. A device made of rubber, felt or similar material for holding a roundel in place in the bezel rings of a signal.

Rounds (Ladder). The horizontal bars on which the foot rests. They are called "rounds" whether made of wood or metal, or whether round or square.

Route. The course or way to be traveled along the railroad or through switches and interlockings.

Route Card Board. A small wooden board secured to the sides and/or ends of a freight car to enable routing instructions, special loading information, or other cards or papers to be attached to the car with tacks or staples.

Route Selection. As applied to automatic switching for classification yards. The term is applied to a desired track destination established for an individual car or cut of cars.

RPM. The common abbreviation for "revolutions per minute," used when referring to the rotational speed of a wheel or shaft.

Rump Rail. In stock car construction, an extra heavy side slat placed about four feet above the floor and running horizontally the length of the car to absorb the major impact of cattle bumping against the car sides.

Run of Pipe. A run of pipe or heater coil is defined as one length of pipe running from one end of the car to the other end of the car.

Running Board. A surface or walkway on cars and locomotives to permit access to hatches, manways or doors, or to facilitate moving on or over the equipment.

Running Gear. A general term used to describe the group of parts whose functions are related to movement of the car. Running gear includes the wheels, axles, bearings, suspensions system and other components of the trucks.

Running Rail. The rail or surface on which the tread of the wheel bears.

Running Repairs. A term describing minor, itemized standard repairs performed and billed by the railroads in accordance with the Interchange Rules.

Running Track. A track reserved for movement through a yard.

Run-Through Train. A train consisting of a solid block of cars handled through a junction point, under an operating agreement, without a scheduled stop other than for necessary change in crew.

S

Saddle. A general term sometimes applied to a bracket or other support used on freight cars, so named because it is made to rest on a curved surface in a way similar to a horse saddle.

Saddleback Car. A specially equipped flatcar provided with folding pedestals at each end of the car, moveable winches, and bridge plates, used for the transportation of highway truck chassis.

Safety Appliance. Any one of several specific components required on railway cars, the functions of which are directly related to the safety of train crew members and other persons whose duties require being on or around the equipment. The design, location, and proper maintenance of safety appliances are strictly regulated by the Department of Transportation. Safety appliances on cars include hand brakes, handholds, ladders, uncoupling levers, sill steps and safety railings.

Safety Tread. Material or coverings for step treads which prevent the foot from slipping.

Safety Valve. A type of pressure relief valve used to protect against an accumulation of excess pressure in a closed vessel.

Safety Vent. An opening formed by a hollow casting or a piece of pipe inserted in the dome of a tank car, used on cars carrying products which are nonflammable or do not give off flammable vapors.

Sampling Line. A device permitting the sampling of the product in a loaded tank car. This line is also known as a "test tube."

Sander. A pneumatic or electric device which applies sand to the rails in front of the driving wheels in order to improve adhesion.

Sand Blast. A process involving the blowing of a pressurized mixture of sand and air onto a surface for the purpose of cleaning rust, old paint or other contaminants from the surface prior to painting. The cleaning medium can also be steel shot or grit, in which case the process is called "shot blasting" or "grit blasting."

Sand Box. A receptacle placed on a locomotive or motor car for carrying sand to prevent slipping of the driving wheels.

Sand Pipe. The tubes leading down from the sand box outlets to the rails in front of the driving wheels.

Scale House. A house to cover the scale beam and providing shelter for the operator of track scales.

Scale Test Car. A car equipped with mechanical appliances for testing the balance of track scales as to their correctness according to the Government Bureau of Standards. See Test Weight Car.

Scale Track. A track leading to and from, and passing over a track scale.

Scale Weight. Weights obtained on railroad scales; the gross, tare and net weight entered on the waybill.

Scarifier. Machine that removes old ballast.

Scavenging (Internal Combustion Engines). The sweeping out of an engine cylinder by piston movement or a blast of air of all or most of the gaseous products of the preceding fuel combustion.

Schedule. A published table of departure and arrival times of arranged service over a specific section of railroad.

Schnabel Car. A specially designed car used for transportation of extremely large and heavy machinery. The car is constructed with two seperate units, each capable of standing alone on its own trucks. The load is placed between the tow carrying units, and rigidly fastened to them, thus becoming literally part of the car body.

Scoring Groove. A groove machined around a tank car outlet valve casing, making a weak point at which failure will occur without damage to the valve seat if the valve becomes overstressed. Also called "breaking groove."

Screw. A cylindrical rod of steel or some other suitable material having helical grooves or threads machined along its length. Depending on the type of thread, screws are used for many purposes including fastening components together, operating machinery or moving heavy objects.

Screw Spike. A cylindrical threaded spike, designed to be turned with a special wrench into holes bored in ties, to secure rails or to act as a tie plate holder in tie plates.

Seal. A general term used to describe any device used to close off completely, to prevent leakage, or to secure. Typical examples of seals found in railroad car work are: air brake valve gaskets, rubber washers in air hose connections, packing in valves and car door seals. See Car Seal.

Seam. A crack on the surface of metal which has been closed but not welded, usually produced by blow holes which have become oxidized.

Seasonal Rate. A rate instituted for specified articles or commodities and effective only certain periods of the year.

Seat. In mechanical systems, a term used to describe a specific location or surface on which another part rests and often depends for proper operation, such as a valve seat.

Section Four Relief. Permission given to the carriers by the Interstate Commerce Commission under certain conditions to publish and charge higher rates for a short haul than for a long haul, when the shorter is contained in the longer.

Section Limits. A division of railroad into specific territories for maintenance purposes. Sections are usually inspected and maintained by an assigned group of men and section limits are usually marked by section posts.

Section Train. Each of two or more trains running on the same timetable schedule at intervals, indicated by designated signals.

Self-Cleaning. A term applied to cars designed to discharge their lading by gravity through bottom or side dumping mechanisms without any external assistance.

Self-Guarded Frog (Flange Frog). A frog provided with guides or flanges, above its running surface, which contact the tread rims of wheels for the purpose of safely guiding their flanges past the frog.

Semaphore Counterweight. A weight so connected that in case of breaking of the pipe controlling the signal, the weight will fall and pull the signal to its most restrictive position.

Semaphore Signal. A signal in which the indications are given by the position of a semaphore arm with or without a light.

Semi-Automatic. A device which is controlled both manually and automatically.

Semiconductors. Materials, such as germanium and silicon, the conductivity of which can be controlled to make devices such as diodes which function as rectifiers.

Semi-Envelope Air Distribution. Air distribution for refrigerator cars in which the cooled or heated air is passed through ducts and flues in ceiling, sides and ends with air return beneath the floor racks on which the lading is placed.

Separator Guard. A metal block of two or more parts acting as a filler between the running rail and the guard rail and so designed as to provide varying widths of flangeways.

Series. A method of connecting electric apparatus so that the negative side of one unit is connected to the positive of the next and the full current passes successively through each piece of apparatus in the circuit. See Parallel.

Series Circuit. A circuit in which the separate sources or separate electro-receptive devices or both are so placed that the current produced in it or going through it passes successively through the entire circuit.

Service Application. A term used to denote a full or normal application of the air brakes on a car or train. A service application is initiated by reducing brake pipe pressure at a rate sufficient to cause the control valve on each car to assume its "service" position and function to cause auxiliary reservoir air to enter the brake cylinder.

Set. The distance a coil spring deflects under load. In an eliptic spring, the set is defined as the distance between the spring bands at the center of the arch. Permanent set is the decrease in free height of any spring that normally occurs over a period of time due to repeated cycles of loading to full travel.

Set-Off. A term descriptive of a car or cars detached from a train enroute between yards or terminals.

Shaft. In construction work, a pit or well sunk from the ground surface above into a tunnel for the purpose of furnishing ventilation or for facilitating the work by increasing the number of points from which it may be carried on. In machinery, a round bar, after iron or steel, usually associated with rotation.

Shaker. A pneumatic or mechanical device which, when attached to shaker plates installed on hopper cars, will vibrate the lading sufficiently to induce unloading.

Shank (of a Coupler). That portion of a coupler between the head and rear surface of the butt.

Shatter Cracks. A rail defect in the form of minute cracks in the interior of rail heads, seldom closer than 1/2 in. from the surface, and visible only after deep etching or at high magnification. They are caused by rapid (air) cooling, and may be prevented from forming by control cooling the rail. Shatter cracks also occur in other steel products.

Shearing Stress. Any force causing two contacting parts or layers to slide upon each other, moving apart in opposite directions parallel to the plane of their contact.

Sheathing. The outside covering of car sides and ends.

Sheave Wheel. A grooved wheel over which a chain, cord or cable runs.

Sheet. The plates used in enclosing all types of steel cars are termed sheets as end sheet, side sheet, roof sheet, floor sheets, etc.

Shelf Coupler. A special coupler, required on some cars designed for transporting hazardous commodities, having top and bottom "shelves" cast integral with the head to prevent vertical disengagement of mating couplers in the event of an excessive end impact. Shelf couplers are fully compatible with other standard A.A.R. couplers. See Head Shield.

Shell Capacity. The capacity of a tank car as measured by the amount of product a tank car contains when the tank shell is completely full.

Shell Innage. A term which designates the depth of the product contained in a tank car.

Shelling. A wheel defect characterized by pieces of metal flaking out of the tread surface, and caused by fatigue failure of the metal in the tread.

Shell Outage. The unfilled portion of a tank car tank as measured by the vertical distance from the underside of the tank shell at the top to the level of product in the tank.

Shim. A thin piece of wood or steel used to properly position one part with respect to another, or to position a complete unit correctly with respect to its supporting or surrounding structure.

Shipper's Load and Count. A phrase appearing on the bill of lading and denoting that the contents of the car were loaded and counted by the shipper and not checked or verified by the carrier. Sometimes designated "Shipper's Load and Tally."

Shipping Order. A shipping order is usually the triplicate copy of the bill of lading containing the shippers' instructions to the carrier for forwarding of goods.

Shoe. In general, any block, plate, or other configuration of material, the function of which involves sliding or rubbing on some other surface. See Brake Shoe and Pantograph.

Short Circuit. A shunt circuit abnormally applied.

Short Line Railroad. A railroad company which may originate or terminate freight traffic on its track, participates in division of revenue and is usually less than 100 miles in length.

Shoulder (Track). That portion of the ballast between the end of the tie and the toe of the ballast slope.

Shove Indicator. A track indicator usually used in a classification yard to indicate that cars have occupied a particular section or sections of a track.

Shrinkage Allowance. The excess length to which a hot rail is cut when leaving the rolls to allow for shrinkage to required length when cold. In a steel casting, the allowance left in the mold for shrinkage of the final product.

Shunt. A bypass, usually controlled by automatic or manual switching devices, to redirect current in an electric circuit.

Shutters. In engine cooling systems, an assembly of movable vanes, mechanically connected to operate in unison that are actuated by a pneumatic magnet valve controlled by an engine temperature switch.

Side Bearing. A load bearing component, located either on the truck or body bolster, and arranged to absorb vertical loads arising from the rocking motion of the car. There are various types of side bearings ranging from simple flat pads to complex devices which maintain constant contact between the truck bolster and car body. See Body Side Bearing and Truck Side Bearing.

Side Bearing Brace. A filler block between the body bolster diaphragms that supports the side bearing.

Side Bearing Clearance. The space between mating body and truck side bearings on cars with conventional side bearing arrangements. The Association of American Railroads has established minimums and maximums for this dimension, when measured on level tangent track.

Side Bearing Roller. A solid steel cylindrical roller which fits loosely in a rectangular retainer or "cage," fastened to the truck bolster, and contacts the body side bearings during lateral rocking of the car. The rollers are used either singly or in pairs, and have the advantage of decreasing resistance to truck rotation when the car is rounding a curve.

Side Door. Any door arrangement in a car side, as distinguished from end doors, drop doors or hopper doors.

Side Dump Car. A car so constructed that its contents may be discharged to either side of the track through doors in the car sides or drop doors in the floor.

Side Frame. In the conventional three-piece truck, the heavy cast steel side member which is designed to transmit vertical loads from the wheels through either journal boxes or pedestals to the truck bolster.

Side Frame Key. A short steel retainer bolted to the bottom of a pedestal type side frame to prevent roller bearing assemblies from becoming dislodged from the side frame pedestals. Sometimes called a Roller Bearing Key.

Side Loading. A method of loading or unloading containers or highway trailers on or off flat cars by physically lifting the unit over the side of the car with heavy duty mobile loading equipment. See Circus Loading.

Side Plate. A structural member of a boxcar side assembly extending the length of the car at the top of the sides, and to which the roof carlines are attached.

Side Sheet. The steel panels fastened to side posts that close in the sides of the car.

Side Sill. The outside longitudinal members of the underframe. In some designs of cars, the side sills are dispensed with and the entire side of the car is designed as a deep plate girder to carry most of the load to the bolster.

Side Stakes. Heavy vertical steel posts that provide the main structural support for hopper or gondola car sides.

Side Track. A track auxiliary to the main track.

Siding. A track auxiliary to the main track for meeting or passing trains. (Standard Code)

Signal, Aspect. See Aspect.

Signal Bridge. A structure constructed to span one or more tracks for the purpose of supporting signals.

Signal Counter. A device for registering the number of signal operations.

Signal Hose. An air hose similar to, but of smaller diameter than, an air brake hose, and used between cars to connect the train air signal lines.

Signal Indication. The information conveyed by the aspect of a signal relative to speed and conditions on the track ahead.

Signal Mast. An upright support from which signals are displayed.

Signalman. A person who maintains and operates railroad signal equipment.

Sill (Construction). The lowest horizontal member of a framed bent.

Sill. The general term used to describe main structural members of of a car underframe. See Center Sill, Side Sill, End Sill.

Sill Step. A steel step fastened to the side sill at each corner of a car to provide footing for employees whose duties require that they be on the equipment. Sill steps are considered safety appliances and are subject to very strict regulation as to their dimensions and location on a car.

Single-Slip Switch. A combination of a crossing and a single connecting track, located within the limits of the crossing, and made up a right-hand switch from the one track and a left-hand switch from the other track, which unite to form the connecting track without additional frogs.

Single Track. One main track on which trains operate in either direction, distinguished from double or multiple track.

Skate. A sliding device placed on a rail to engage with a car wheel so as to provide continuous braking by sliding friction.

Skate Machine. A mechanism electrically controlled and electrically or pneumatically operated, for placing a skate on, or removing it from the rail.

Skeletonized Track. Track where the ballast is removed from the cribs between the ties.

Skirt (of a Piston). The lower portion of the piston.

Slabbed Tie. A tie sawed on top and bottom only. Also known as "pole tie" and "round tie."

Slack. Unrestrained free movement between the cars in a train.

Slack Adjuster. A device installed in the foundation brake rigging of a railway car, usually near the brake cylinder live lever, used to automatically compensate for variations in the brake rigging caused by brake shoe and wheel wear or replacement. The slack adjuster functions to take up rigging slack as wear occurs, or to let out slack when new shoes or wheels are applied. Brake cylinder piston travel is thereby automatically maintained at its optimum length without the need for manual brake rigging adjustments.

Slag. A non-metallic fused product which results from the reduction of ore in a furnace, or the fusion of metal in a welding operation.

Slide Fence. A wire fence constructed along the railroad in slide-prone areas, which acts as a warning device because it is connected to signals which will stop a train in advance of meeting an obstruction on the track caused by a rock slide.

Sliding Door. A door which opens by moving sideways instead of swinging on hinges.

Sliding Sill. A term used to describe a type of hydraulic cushioning for freight car underframes. In sliding sill designs, a single hydraulic unit is installed at the center of the car and acts to control longitudinal forces received at either end of an auxiliary center sill, which is free to travel longitudinally within a fixed center sill.

Slope Sheet. In hopper car construction, the steel sheets that slope from the sides and ends to form the hoppers in the bottom of the car.

Slot. A disconnecting device inserted in the connection between a signal arm and its operating mechanism.

Slot Weld. A weld made in an elongated slot through one member of a lap joint.

Slow Speed. A speed governed by timetable instructions and related to various signal indications as defined in the operating rules of a particular railroad.

Slug. A cabless locomotive which has traction motors, but no means of supplying power to them by itself. Power is provided by power cables from an adjacent unit. Slugs are used where low speeds and high tractive effort are needed, such as in hump yards.

Smoke Jack. A term commonly applied to the outside portion of a smoke flue when used on caboose and work cars.

Snow Crab. A car equipped at its rear end with high, vertically-hinged side wings, adaptable to being spread to cut into deep snow on each side of the track with the vertical cutting edges of their divergent braced surfaces, in order to draw the snow in between the rails behind the car, whence it may be handled with a following rotary plow, thus widening the snow cut.

Snow Fence. A structure erected for the purpose of forming artificial eddies on the windward side of a cut at sufficient distance away to cause snow to deposit between the snow fence and the cut.

Snow Melter. Equipment used for melting snow with an open flame, used at interlocking plants and yards to clear track switches during and after a snow storm.

Snow Plow. A unit of maintenance of way equipment designed to remove snow from railroad tracks. The two most common types are the wedge plow and the rotary plow.

Snow Sweeper. A car equipped with brushes, near the rails, and the necessary machinery to revolve them; used for sweeping snow from the rails.

Snubbers. Hydraulic or friction damping devices used in suspension systems of cars to improve lateral stability. Some snubbers are designed to replace one spring in the truck spring group, some are incorporated as part of the truck side frame or bolster design, and others require special installation. Supplemental hydraulic snubbing is used most often on cars with high centers of gravity such as 100 ton coal hoppers or gondolas, and tri-level automobile rack cars.

Soaking Pit (Steelmaking). A vertical reheating furnace in which the ingots, after being stripped, are placed in an upright position for the purpose of uniformly reheating them to the temperature required for rolling.

Socket Washer. A large washer with a cavity to receive the head or nut of a bolt or rod so that it will not project beyond the surface to which it is attached. Also called "cup washer."

Soffit. The underside of a beam, slab, arch, lintel or other projection.

Solenoid. A coil of insulated copper wire wound on a spool which, when an electric current flows through the wire may draw or attract an iron rod, core or plunger into its interior. A modified form of electromagnet. Used as a means for operating regulators, switches and other electrical apparatus.

Solid Bottom Car. Usually an open top gondola car without openings in the floor or bottom for discharging the load.

Solid Wire. Wire made from a single solid strand as opposed to braided wire, which is composed of many fine strands twisted together.

Sorting Yard. A yard in which cars are classified in greater detail after having passed through a classification yard.

Span Bolster. A beam-like structure with each end resting on a conventional truck bolster and arranged to support a car body through a center plate at or near its mid point. Span bolsters can also be used with two six-wheel trucks to provide 24-wheel (12 axle) support under extremely heavy cars.

Spanner. A wrench for uncoupling hose, etc., formed like the arc of a circle, with notches or lugs, for engaging grooves on a spanner nut.

Spark Arrester. A cage-like device of rust-resistant perforated sheets, wire, or expanded metal installed in the flue at the top of an exhaust stack or chimney, the purpose of which is to reduce the hazard from flying sparks.

Spark Gap. The space through which a disrupted discharge passes.

Special Trackwork. All rails, track structures and fittings, other than plain unguarded track that is neither curved nor fabricated before laying.

Special Train. A train not regularly scheduled and operated for a special party, movement or excursion.

Specification. Detailed requirements that a design, product, device or facility must meet to be eligible for A.A.R. approved status. These requirements may pertain to performance, methods of fabrication, material, quality control, laboratory and field test procedures, or other criteria. (A.A.R.)

Specific Gravity. A ratio of the weight of a given solid or liquid to the weight of an equal volume of water under specified standard condition. Materials with specific gravities less than 1.0 will float on water and those with specific gravities greater than 1.0 will sink.

Spectacle. That part of a semaphore signal which holds the roundels and to which the blade is fastened.

Speed Control. A device which will automatically apply the brakes on the train or engine unless the speed conforms to the cab signal indication.

Speed Recorder. A device, usually driven from an axle of a truck, which indicates and records the speed of a train. Business cars, dynamometer cars and locomotives are equipped with speed recorders.

Spike. A long steel square nail with a cutting edge used to secure rail in place.

Spike Puller. A tool with a claw end and two or three pairs of knobs on a straight bar used to withdraw spikes.

Spiked Switch. A switch whose points are held in fixed position by a spike to prevent the switch from being thrown or to prevent trains from using a track that has been taken out of service.

Spiral. When used with respect to track; a form of easement curve in which the change of degree of curve is uniform throughout its length.

Spiral Elliptic Spring. A spring made of a thin band of steel wound in a spiral coil, the transverse section of which is elliptical.

Splice Bar. A steel bar used to fasten together the ends of rails. Used in pairs, one on each side of the rail; and are designed to fit the space between head and base closely. They are held in place by track bolts and suitable accessory equipment. Also called "joint bars," or "fishplates."

Splice Drilling. The spacing of holes in the ends of rails or other track structures to receive the bolts for the fastening of joint bars.

Splice Plate. A steel plate usually of some specified dimension, spanning a break or a joint in some structural member, and securely fastened (usually welded) to both parts so as to form a continuous member.

Split Reduction. A term describing a method of making an air brake application (brake pipe reduction) in two or more steps to produce smoother stopping.

Split Switch. A track structure consisting of two movable point rails and necessary fixtures used to divert rolling stock from one track to another.

Split Switch (Slang). A term referring to the condition that exists at a switch when one pair of wheels under a car follows a course different from all other wheels under the car, generally resulting in a derailment. The errant wheels are said to have "picked" the switch.

Split Web. A longitudinal or diagonal transverse crack in the web of a rail.

Spot Board (Trackwork). A sighting board placed above and across the track at the proposed height to indicate the new surface and ensure its uniformity.

Spotting. The act of placing a car in a specific location on a track.

Spot Weighing. The weighing of a car which is not coupled to other cars.

Spot Weld (Structures). A weld made by fusing parts together under pressure when heated by a localized current; used chiefly in pressed-steel work.

Spreader A piece of maintenance of way equipment having plow-type blades for distributing ballast on the roadbed. The term spreader is also used to refer to the connection between the two vertical truck levers in truck brake rigging. See Bottom Rod.

Spring. A general term referring to a large group of mechanical devices making use of the elastic properties of materials to cushion loads or control motion. See Coil Spring, Elliptic Spring, Truck Spring, and Volute Spring.

Spring Band. A metal strap which embraces the plates or leaves at the center of an elliptic spring.

Spring Cap. A cup-shaped piece of cast or wrought iron for holding the top of a spring and against which the latter bears. They are further distinguished by the name of the spring, such as bolster spring cap, etc.

Spring Clip. The cap or fastener at the ends of elliptical springs. Also called "spring block."

Spring Dampener. A device to increase the capacity of a spring by bringing into play a certain amount of friction which helps to absorb the load or shock.

Spring Group. Any combination of standardized coil springs used in each truck side frame, and selected to match car capacities and obtain desired vertical suspension characterisitcs. Cars are often stenciled to show the number of specific springs of various designations, e.g., 5 D5 outer 3 D5 inner, that make up the spring group standard to the car.

Spring Leaf. The principal component of an elliptic or semi-elliptic spring. They are made of flat spring steel in varying lengths, held together at the center by a band.

Spring Nest. Two or more coil springs of different diameters, one fitting inside the other and acting in combination. Truck springs are commonly made up of standardized outer and inner coils, nested and arranged in various spring groups.

Spring Plank. A steel plate fitting under each end of the truck bolster on older trucks to provide a bearing surface for the spring group.

Spring Plate. A common term for spring seats and caps, especially those of considerable size, as for bolster springs. They are often provided with spring plate lugs to hold the spring in place.

Spring Seat. A cup-shaped piece of cast steel, or cast wrought iron, on which the bottom of a spring rest. Also called "spring plate." They are further distinguished by the name of the spring for which they serve such as bolster spring seat, equalizer spring seat. See Spring Cap.

Spring Switch. A track switch with a spring mechanism that automaticially returns the switch points to a normal position after they have been displaced by passage of cars in a trailing point movement.

Spring Washer. A member designed to prevent backward movement of the nut and looseness in the bolted members of a rail joint, due to wear, stretch, rust or other deterioration.

Spur Track. As distinguished from a side track, a spur track is of indefinite length, extending out from main line.

Squeeze Out. A term generally used in conjuction with retarders, having reference to a situation where a car wheel or wheels are lifted off the track and ride the retarder brake shoes due to excessive pressure.

SS Protection. An arrangement of circuits whereby proceed aspects of a signal cannot be displayed unless a switch and its controlling lever or equivalent device are in corresponding positions.

Staggers Rail Act of 1980. An act of Congress which fundamentally altered the regulatory environment of the railroad industry by reducing regulations including the elimination of antitrust immunity in certain areas of activity.

Staff. The part of the apparatus used in a train staff system, the possession of which gives the train permission to enter a block.

Staff Crane. A structure for supporting train staff for delivery to a train.

Staff Tip Adapter. A device mounted on the tip of a staff of a switch stand for applying switch lamp to the stand.

Stake. A piece of timber or metal bar inserted in a pocket on the sides and ends of flatcars to hold the load in place.

Stake Pocket A "U" shaped collar attached to the side or end sill of a flat car to receive the lower end of a stake used for securing open top loads.

Stanchion. See Trailer Hitch.

Standard (A.A.R.). A specification, procedure, practice, definition, design, product or device which is approved by the A.A.R. to serve as the requirement for use in unrestricted interchange service.

Standard Code. The operating, block signal and interlocking rules of the Association of American Railroads.

Standard Clock. A clock designated in the timetable which indicates standard time, and against which operating employees must check their watches before going on duty.

Standard Gage. The standard distance between rails of North American railroads, being 4' 8-1/2" measured between the inside faces of the rail heads.

Standard Level. A term refering to the deck height of many intermodal and automobile rack flatcars, to differentiate them from so-called low level cars. Standard level cars have a deck height of 41-1/2" as opposed to the 31-1/2" deck height of low level cars.

Standard Transportation Commodity Code (STCC). A seven-digit number assigned to every commodity shipped in transporation.

Standing Yard Capacity. The sum of the capacities of all the tracks in a yard on which cars may be permitted to stand.

Standpipe. A tank in which the bottom is located at or near the surface of the ground, the interior of the entire structure being utilized for the storage of water.

Star Symbol. A term sometimes used to describe the star stenciled immediately to the left of capacity and/or load limit markings on freight cars to indicate that the starred figures have been reduced below those normally expected for the size of journal bearings and axles under the car. Starred capacity and load limit figures must not be changed without authority from the car owner.

Static Head. The difference in elevation between the surface of the water at the source of supply and the elevation at any given point.

Station. A place designated in the time-table by name. (Standard Code)

Station Track. A track upon which trains are placed to receive or discharge passengers, baggage, mail and express.

Steam Generator. For heating passenger cars and operating steam ejector type of air conditioning, a boiler is applied to passenger diesel locomotives. They are generally equipped with an automatic oil fired burner and function without any attention except to start and stop them.

Steam Jacket. An enclosure around a pipe, tank or nozzle to enable steam to be injected and circulated around the equipment to facilitate flow of the product within the system.

Steam Trap. A device for catching and liberating the water of condensation in any steam pipe line.

Steeple Cab. Electric locomotive with cab in center and sloping hoods at each end.

Stenciling. A term used to describe all forms of lettering on cars regardless of the actual method of application.

Step. A general term to describe any one of many arrangements providing a place to stand or to place one's foot. See Brake Step, Sill Step, etc.

Step Riser. The vertical portion of a step in stairs.

Stile. The upright pieces on the outer edge of a door, sash, or ladder.

Stirrup. A bent bar of steel resembling somewhat the stirrup of a saddle and used to support another piece.

Stock Car. A rail car designed for the transportation of livestock and equipped with slatted sides and doors.

Stock-Guard. A barrier of wood, metal or other material, placed between and along side of track rails, to prevent livestock from wandering on or along the track.

Stock Rail. The rail against which the point of a switch, derail or movable point frog rests.

Stop-Off (Tariff). A privilage afforded shippers on carload freight shipments at stations between points of origin and final destination, for the purpose of finishing loading or partly unloading, or taking advantage of transit or other privileges permitted in accordance with tariff rules and regulations.

Stopping Distance. The maximum distance on any portion of any railroad which any train operating on such portion of railroad at its maximum authorized speed will travel during a full service application of the brakes, between the point where such application is initiated and the point where the train comes to a stop. (I.C.C.)

Storage (In-Transit). Stopping of goods at a place located between the points of origin and destination for the purpose of storage.

Storage Track. A track on which cars are placed when held awaiting disposition or when not in service.

Straight-Air Brake. An obsolete type of air brake equipment for railroad cars, but used extensively as the independent brake or locomotive. Air is admitted directly to the brake cylinder by the brake valve in a brake system. See Automatic Air Brake.

Strain. The incremental change in dimensions of a member subjected to stress.

Stranded Wire. Wire made up of many fine strands twisted together.

Strap Bolt. A round bolt with a flat bar of iron or steel welded to it, and usually with a hook on the end which serves as a head. The flat bar has holes in it, by which it can be fastened in place with rivets, bolts, or screws. Also called "lug bolt."

Strap Washer. An iron or steel strap which takes the heads of several bolts. Also called "washer plate."

Stress. A term used in engineering to denote force per unit of area in structural members, expressed commonly in units of lbs. per sq. inch, and abbreviated psi. Stresses are classified by the type of reaction they produce in the fibers of the material they affect. Tensile stress tends to pull apart, compressive stress tends to press together, and sheer stress tends to slide paralled adjacent surfaces against each other in opposite directions.

Striker. The heavy cast, forged, or fabricated bar fastened to the end of the center sill at the top, and designed to be the first point of contact in the event the car coupler is driven back far enough to strike the car body. Its function is to absorb the resulting impact and prevent damage to the center sill and surrounding area.

Stringer. A longitudinal member of a car underframe usually designed to be a floor support rather than to perform the function of a sill.

String Lining. A method of determining the corrections to be made in the alignment of a curve, by measuring ordinates to the outer rail.

Stroke (Internal Combustion Engines). The distance that a piston moves from one end of its path to the other. The piston stroke is equal to twice the length of the crankarm.

Strut. A term applied to any member of a structure normally subjected to compressive stresses.

Stub Sill. A short longitudinal structural member of a car underframe designed to accommodate the coupler and draft gear, and to transmit coupler forces to the car body on cars designed with no through center sill. Common stub sill applications are found on tank and covered hopper cars.

Stub Station. One in which the station tracks are connected at one end only.

Stub Track. A form of side track connected to a running track at one end only and usually protected at the end by some form of bumping post or other solid obstruction.

Stud. A headless bolt either welded or otherwise secured to some component, and used for attaching an adjoining component by means of threaded nut.

Stuffing Box. An enclosure containing packing to prevent leakage around a machine part.

Subballast. Any material which is spread on the finished subgrade of the roadbed below the top-ballast to provide better drainage, prevent upheaval by frost, and better distribute the load over the roadbed.

Subdrain. A covered drain, below the roadbed or ground surface, receiving water along its length through perforations or joints.

Subgrade. The finished surface of the roadbed below the ballast and track.

Subway Car. An electric motor car for use in rapid transit service in large.

Suction Pipe. A line of pipe through which a pump draws its supply.

Sump. A small depression located near the longitudinal center of a tank bottom.

Sun Kink. A small irregularity in track alignment which is caused by excessive compression in the rails.

Supercharger. An exhaust-gas turbine and a centrifugal blower or compressor mounted on a common rotor shaft which delivers air to an engine at a pressure above atmospheric. Turbine utilizes energy in the exhaust from the engine to operate the compressor.

Superelevation. The vertical distance the outer rail is raised above the inner rail on curves to resist the centrifugal force of moving trains.

Superliners. Bi-level passenger cars operated by AMTRAK on long distance service.

Supply Pipe (Air Compressor). A pipe sometimes connected to the air inlet of an air compressor by means of which the air supply is drawn from a point some distance away from the compressor.

Suppression. A position on the quadrant of the 26C Automatic Brake Valve in which the handle must be placed to recover from a penalty brake application. This is also a feature used to prevent an automatic train control brake application.

Surface (Track). The condition of the track as to vertical evenness or smoothness.

Surplus Cars. Empty revenue freight cars not in transit; including cars stored for special or future loading, in excess of shippers' orders for cars.

Suspension. The resilent system through which a car body is supported on its wheels. Suspension systems involve the use of hydraulic devices, friction elements and coil, elliptic, rubber or pneumatic springs.

Swing Bolster. A truck bolster suspended by hangers or links so that it can swing laterally with relation to the truck and thus lower the effects of lateral impact received through the side frames and wheels. Trucks equipped with swing bolsters are known as swing motion trucks.

Swing Hanger. Bars or links, attached at their upper ends to the frame of a swing motion truck, and carrying the spring plank at their lower ends. Also called "bolster hanger."

Swing Motion Truck. A truck with a bolster and spring plank suspended on swing hangers so that they can swing laterally in relation to the truck frame.

Switch. A track structure with movable rails to divert rolling stock from one track to another.

Switch Angle. The angle included between the gage lines or the switch rail at its point and the stock rail.

Switch Adjustment Bracket. A bracket attached to the No. 1 rod to which the operating rod is connected, and which permits the adjustment of a switch, derail or movable point frog.

Switch-and-Lock Movement. A device, the complete operation of which performs the three functions of unlocking, operating, and locking a switch, movable point frog, or derail. (I.C.C.)

Switch Clip. The device that attaches the switch rod to the switch rail. Horizontal switch clips allow the switch rod to lay with its broad side horizontally. Vertical switch clips position the broad side vertically. Both types allow rotation of the points with reference to the clips.

Switch, Electro-Pneumatic. A track switch operated by an electro-pneumatic switch-and-lock movement.

Switcher. A term used for a switching locomotive.

Switch, Facing Point. A track switch, the points of which face traffic approaching in the direction for which the track is signaled.

Switch Guard. A rail or other track structure laid parallel with the running rail ahead of a split switch and forming a flangeway with the running rail, to hold the wheels of rolling stock in correct alignment when approaching the switch.

Switch, Hand-Operated. A non-interlocked track switch which can only be operated manually. (I.C.C.)

Switch Heater. Heater used to keep switches warm enough to prevent "freeze up".

Switch Heel. That end of a switch rail which is the farther from its point, and nearer the frog.

Switch Indicator. An indicator used at a non-interlocked switch to indicate the condition of a block.

Switching. Switching service consists of moving cars from one track to another track or to different positions on the same track. It includes the moving of cars in the make-up and break-up of trains; also moving of cars on industrial switching tracks or interchange tracks, and the general movement of cars within terminals or at junctions.

Switching and Terminal Companies. Carriers performing primarily switching service, or terminal service at stations, stockyards, etc.

Switching Charge. The rate or charge for a switching service, made usually on flat per car basis or on so much per hundredweight or ton.

Switching Limits. The extent of the area within which cars are moved under switching rules and charges.

Switching Locomotive. A locomotive used for shifting or switching cars in yards and terminals. Sometimes termed "switcher."

Switching Tariff. A schedule containing charges for switching.

Switch, Insulated. A switch in which the fixtures, principally in gage plates and the switch rods connecting one rail to the other, are provided with insulation so that electric currents will not be shunted. Also, the turnout rail contains an insulating joint.

Switch, Interlocked. A track switch within the interlocking limits, the control of which is interlocked with other functions of the interlocking.

Switch Lamp. A mechanically rotated electric light unit, supplementing the switch target, for indicating position of switch or derail.

Switch Machine. A machine used to throw track switches. There are both automatic and manual switch machines.

Switchman. A yard brakeman.

Switch Plate. A special metal tie plate for use on switch ties.

Switch Point. A movable tapered track rail, the point of which is designed to fit against the stock rail.

Switch Point Protector. A device which engages the wheel and deflects it away from the switch point.

Switch Rail Brace. A metal shape designed to fit the contour of the side of the stock rail and extend over the switch plate, with provision for fastening through the plate to the tie, to restrain the movement of the stock rail.

Switch Rod. A rod connecting the two points of a switch or movable point frog, by means of which the relative distance between the points is maintained.

Switch Signal. A low two-indication horizontal color light signal with electric lamps, for indicating position of switch or derail.

Switch Stand. A device for the manual operation of switches, or of movable center points.

Switch Tie. The transverse member of the track structure which is longer than, but fuctions as does the cross tie, and in addition supports a crossover or turnout.

Swivel Butt Coupler. An obsolete coupler design in which the solid shank was replaced by a swiveling butt casting connected to the coupler itself by means of a pin.

T

Take Siding Indicator. An indicator generally used to convey instructions to approaching trains to take siding.

Tally Card. A card or envelope provided to facilitate check of passengers on train by the conductor and crew.

Tamper. A power-driven machine for compacting ballast under ties.

Tamping Bar. A steel bar with a blade on each end used to drive ballast beneath the ties.

Tangent. Any straight portion of a railway alinement. Tangent track means straight track with no curves.

Tank Anchor. Longitudinal steel sections fastened to the center sill which are in turn fastened to the tank to anchor it to the underframe at the center of the car.

Tank Band. An iron strap which passes around the tank of a tank car to hold it in place on the underframe of tank cars using this arrangement.

Tank Car. A rail car, the body of which consists of a tank for transporting liquids. Tank cars may be pressure or non-pressure, and are often equipped with special equipment to enhance their usefulness for handling specific commodities.

Tank Dome. A vertical cylinder attached to the top of a tank car. It permits the tank proper to be filled to full cubical capacity, which would be impossible if there were no dome.

Tank Head. The circular, curved and/or elliptical pressed end sheet of a cylindrical tank.

Tank Outlet (or Nozzle). A short pipe used to empty a tank. It is usually cast in one piece with the tank valve seat.

Tank Outlet Cap. A screwed fitting attached to the bottom of a tank outlet for the purpose of closing it tightly.

Tank Saddle. The bearing structure which supports the tank. On some tank cars the saddle is also part of the body bolster.

Tank Valve. A valve attached to the bottom of the tank to draw off the contents.

Taper. The difference in brake pipe pressure between the front and rear of the train with all equipment fully charged.

Tare Weight. As applied to a carload, weight of the car exclusive of its contents.

Target. An indicating device on a track switch, mechanically actuated by a switch stand, or a switch point, to indicate the position of the switch. Some switch targets are reflectorized to enable night visibility.

Tariff (Freight). A schedule containing matter relative to transportation movements, rates, rules and regulations.

Tariff Circulars (I.C.C.). Circulars issued by the Interstate Commerce Commission containing rules and regulations to be observed by the carriers in the publication, construction and filing of tariffs and other schedules.

Team Track. A track on which rail cars are placed for the use of the public in loading or unloading freight.

Templet or Template. A gage for checking the shape and size of a rail section.

Tension Member. Any structural member subjected to a tensile stress, such as the top cover plate of a built-up body bolster.

Terminal. A railroad facility used for handling of passengers or freight and the receiving, classifying, assembling, and dispatching of trains.

Terminal Board. A slab or board on which wire terminals are mounted.

Terminal Charge. A charge assessed for services performed at terminals.

Terminal Junction Point. Important commercial points at which carriers maintain terminal facilities for interchange of freight between gateways and local area points.

Terminal Switching. Car movements wholly within switching or yard limits.

Test Weight Car. A specially constructed car having a precisely known weight and used to verify the accuracy of railway scales.

TGV. Abbreviation for "tres grande vitesse" (French). Translated, it means, "very high speed train."

Thermal Cracking. A wheel defect characterized by fine cracks running transversely across the tread and caused by excessive heat generated at the tread surface during heavy prolonged braking. Undetected thermal cracks will propagate through the flange or rim into the wheel plate and cause failure.

Thermit Weld. A weld made by pouring molten materials into the gap between rail ends which fuses to the rail ends, eliminating the need for joint bars.

Thermostat. A device to control operation of equipment in response to changes in temperature.

Thimble. The cylindrical piece of an insulating joint which surrounds a portion of the bolt.

Third-Rail. A current distribution system for electric railroads consisting of an insulated rail laid parallel to one of the running rails and arranged to provide a continuous supply of power to electric locomotives.

Third-Rail Clearance Line. The contour that embraces all cross sections of third rail and its insulators, supports, and guards located at an elevation higher than the top of the running rail.

Third-Rail Shoe. A metallic sliding contact attached to the trucks of electric traction equipment for the purpose of collecting current from the third-rail distribution system.

Three-Stem Platform Equipment. The conventional arrangement of buffing mechanism used in passenger train cars. It consists of a center stem within the platform, between the buffer plate and the buffing gear, which absorbs the buffing shocks. This is aided by two side stems and springs which act to keep the buffer plate in proper alignment.

Threshold Plate. In boxcar construction, a formed structural member extending across the door opening at the floor, and fitted at the door posts.

Throat. In car wheel nomenclature, the term used to refer to the area around the radius formed at the junction of the wheel flange and the wheel tread.

Throat. In track nomenclature, the point where the converging wings of a frog are closest together just ahead of the frog point.

Throttle. The regulating handle and connections that determine the amount of fuel entering an engine, thereby determining the engine and locomotive speed.

Through Freight Train. An express freight train between major terminals.

Through Rate. A rate applicable from point of origin to its destination. It consists of two or more separately established rates added together to make a total charge for a through haul, and operating as a unit for a single transportation service and on a through bill of lading. See Joint Rate.

Through Station. One in which the station tracks continue past the station and are connected at both ends.

Thrust Collar. A collar fastened to a shaft or axle by means of a set screw to prevent its shifting endwise.

Tie. In structures, a beam or rod which secures parts together and is subjected to a tensile stress. In track construction, the cross members to which the rails are attached. See Railroad Tie.

Tie Down. Any device for securing a load to the deck of a car. Chain tie downs with ratchets are probably the most common type and are used to secure wheeled vehicles and lumber products on flat cars.

Tie Pad. A cushioning device located between the rail and the tie (mainly used on bridges).

Tie Plate. A steel plate interposed between a rail or other track structure and a tie.

Tie Plug. Rectangular sections of wood, shaped somewhat like spikes, for driving into holes from which spikes have been withdrawn.

Tie Rod. When used without specific reference, any rod or thin beam in a structure used to connect two other parts of the structure. Tie rods are usually, but not always, in tension.

Tight-Lock Coupler. A special coupler for passenger cars that minimized slack for smoother train handling.

Time-Table. A published schedule of the movement of trains.

Timing. The regular action of mechanically opening and closing the valves on an internal combustion engine. The movement is "timed" to coincide with events occurring in each cylinder and is controlled by the cam shaft.

Tipple. A track beneath or beside conveyor belts or bins that load ore, rock, coal or other material into open-top cars.

Toe (of a Frog). End of a frog nearest the switch.

TOFC. An acronym for "trailer on flatcar" intermodal service.

Tolerance. The allowable variation from specified dimensions on a drawing.

Ton-Mile. A term denoting the transportation of one ton of freight a distance of one mile. Ton-miles contemplate the multiplication of the weight in tons of each shipment transported by the distance hauled.

Top-Ballast. Any material spread over a subballast to support the track structure, distribute the load to the subballast, and provide a good initial drainage.

Top Chord. The upper structural member of the side or end of an open top car, usually designed as a heavy channel or angle to withstand high bending stresses.

Top Plate. One of the three primary components of a trailer hitch. The top plate is the horizontal component that contacts the trailer fifth wheel and secures the kingpin in any one of several jaw mechanisms. The top plate is sometimes known as the "head weldment."

Top Rod. In freight car foundation brake rigging, the brake rod that connects the truck live lever to the body rigging system.

Torpedo. An explosive cap fastened to the top of the rail and exploded by the pressure of a rolling wheel to give an audible indication of conditions on the track ahead.

Torque. A term used to describe the twisting force required to turn a bolt or a rotating shaft. Torque is measured in units of foot pounds (ft. lbs.) or inch pounds (in. lbs.) and is calculated by multiplying the applied force (in pounds) by the distance to its point of application (in feet or inches).

Tower Car. A rail vehicle, the propulsion of which is effected by electric means and that is provided with an elevated platform, generally arranged to be raised and lowered, for the installation, inspection, and repair of a contact wire system.

Tracer (Cable). One of the wires in a cable marked in such a manner as to readily distinguished from the other wires.

Track. An assembly of rails, ties and fastenings over which cars, locomotives and trains are moved.

Trackage Rights. The right of one carrier to use track owned by another carrier pursuant to an agreement between them.

Track Bolt. A bolt with a button head and oval, or elliptical neck, and a threaded nut designed to fasten together rails and joint bars.

Track Brace. A fastening designed to brace the rail on the high side of a curve.

Track Capacity. The number of cars that can stand in the clear on any given track.

Track Car. Any equipment operated on track, such as motor car, hand car, trailer, or other unit not on standard railcar trucks.

Track Centers. The distance, measure at right angles, between center lines of parallel tracks.

Track Chart. A map-like representation of the grade and alignment of a section of a railroad.

Track Circuit. An electrical circuit of which the rails of the track form a part. (I.C.C.)

Track Circuit Connector. A device used for connecting one or more wires to a rail.

Track Crossing. A structure which permits one track to cross another at grade consisting of four connected frogs.

Track Element. That portion of the roadway apparatus of automatic train stop, train control or cab signal system, such as electric circuit, inductor, magnet, ramp or trip arm to which the locomotive apparatus of such system is directly responsive. (I.C.C)

Track Fullness. A term referring to amount of space, in terms of car lengths (figured at average specified length per car), available on a classification track of a classification yard usually measured from the clearance point of a classification track in a direction away from apex of hump.

Track Gage. A device by which the gage of a track is established or measured.

Track Indicator Chart. A map-like reproduction of railway tracks controlled by track circuits so arranged as to indicate automatically, for defined sections of track, whether or not such sections are occupied.

Track Layout. A diagram of the physical location of tracks in a yard or terminal.

Track Relay. A relay receiving all or part of its operating energy through conductors of which the track rails are an essential part.

Track Scale. A scale especially designed for weighing railway equipment.

Track Shims. Flat wood boards of length and width similar to tie plates. They are placed between the ties and the tie plates when the ballast is frozen to correct surface irregularities.

Track-Train Dynamics. The study of the motions and resulting forces that occur during the movement of a train over a track under varying conditions of speed, train makeup, track and equipment conditions, grades, curves and train handling.

Traction Motor. A specially designed direct current series-wound motor mounted on the trucks of locomotives and self-propelled cars to drive the axles.

Tractive Effort. The useable force exerted by the wheels of a locomotive at the rails for pulling a train.

Traffic Control System. A block signal system under which train movements are authorized by block signals whose indications supersede the superiority of trains for both opposing and following movements on the same track. (I.C.C.)

Traffic Lever. A lever, or equivalent controlling device, used as a check lever, crossing lever, detector lever, master lever, route lever; also to control another lever, group of levers or functions to establish traffic direction.

Trailer. A cargo carrying highway vehicle without automotive power. Trailers are usually hauled by a powered vehicle called a tractor. Trailers became of major importance to the railroad industry with the introduction of piggyback or TOFC service.

Trailer Car. A four-wheeled work car equipped with a seat, foot boards, safety rails and brakes. Used for transporting men, and may be converted into a push car by removing the seat, foot boards and railings.

Trailer Hitch. A specially designed device mounted on a TOFC car for the purpose of supporting and securing highway trailers during rail transit. Trailer hitches may either be rigid or cushioned, and they may or may not be retractable, depending on their intended service.

Trailing Movement. The movement of a train over the points of a switch which face in the direction in which the train is moving. (I.C.C.)

Trailing Point Switch. A track switch, the points of which face away from traffic approaching in the direction for which the track is signaled.

Trailing Unit. See "B" Unit.

Train. An engine or more than one engine coupled, with or without cars, displaying markers. For practical purposes, a train is a group of coupled cars hauled by a locomotive.

TRAIN. The name given to a computerized car movement system coordinated by the Association of American Railroads for furnishing information to member railroads about movement of their cars throughout the country.

Train Air Signal. In passenger trains, a means of signaling the locomotive engineman from any car in the train using a separate air line (the signal line) connected between the cars and running the length of the train. Operation of a conductor's valve, usually located in the vestibule of each car, causes a high pitched "beep" tone in the locomotive cab, alerting the engineman to take some predetermined action.

Train Blocking. An operating term used to describe the sorting and pre-grouping of cars for movement in a train according to their intended destination (or intermediate terminal) to minimize enroute switching.

Train-Contol Territory. That portion of a railroad equipped with an automatic train-control system. See Automatic Train-Control.

Train Line. A term properly applied to describe the continuous line of brake pipe extending from the locomotives to the last car in a train, with all cars and air hoses coupled. The term is often used to refer to the brake pipe on a single car.

Trainman. A persons who assists the conductor.

Train Order. An order issued by or through a proper railway official to govern the movements of a train.

Train Order Signal. A signal used to indicate to a train whether or not it will receive orders.

Train Resistance. The combined effect of friction, grade, curves and wind that tend to resist the effort exerted by the locomotive to move a train.

Train Staff Pusher Attachment. An attachment to electric train staff apparatus, designed to protect (in addition to the regular train movement) the movement of a pusher engine when it is to be run back to its starting point after being detached from the rear of the train.

Transfer Table. A device for transferring cars from one track to another parallel track, consisting of a bridge-like structure carrying a section of track, and fitted with flanged wheels at each end that roll on steel rails laid along either side of a long pit.

Transformer. An electrical device to increase or decrease voltage in an A.C. circuit.

Transit. The terms "transit privilege" and "transit arrangement" have reference to milling-in-transit, fabrication, dressing lumber in transit, etc., but do not cover straight carload shipment diverted, reconsigned, stopped in transit to partly unload or to add to load.

Transit Charge. A charge limited in its application to traffic which has been or will be milled, stored, or otherwise specially treated enroute.

Transit Point. The point where transit privileges are provided.

Transit Privileges. Privileges granted to shippers with respect to goods in transit whereby the goods may be further processed at intermediate points and continue to destination with the through rate being protected.

Transit Rate. A rate restricted in its application to traffic which has been or will be milled, stored or otherwise specially treated in transit.

Transition. Changes in a Diesel electric locomotive's traction motor circuits from series, to series-parallel, to parallel, to enable the locomotive to operate within the limits of its speed range without overloading the electrical equipment.

Transverse Fissure. A rail defect originating inside the rail head and spreading outward, crosswise of the rail.

Trap. In pipe fitting work, an arrangement in a pipeline to catch or retain a portion of the fluid flowing in the system.

Trap Door. A door in a floor or roof, closing flush when shut. On passenger cars, a door over the steps in the vestibule, making a full width platform when the door is closed.

Tread. In car wheel nomenclature, the slightly tapered exterior running surface of the wheel that comes in contact with the top surface of the rail, and also serves as a brake drum on cars with conventional brake arrangements. In rail nomenclature, the top surface of the rail which contacts the vehicle.

Treated Ties. Cross, switch, or bridge ties subjected to a preservative process such as creosoting.

Trickle Charge. A continuous input of current to a storage battery to compensate for internal losses only.

Tri-Level Car. A flatcar designed with integral superstructure of posts, bracings and decking to permit triple level loading of automobiles. The deck of the underframe serves as the lower deck of the superstructure.

Trimmer. A signal located near the summit in a hump yard, which gives indication concerning movement from the classification tracks toward the summit.

Trolley. A term referring to an overhead electric contact wire on electric railroads or transit systems.

Trolley Car. An electric motor car that collects propulsion power from a trolley system.

Trolley Shoe. A sliding metallic contact piece for collecting current from an overhead wire. Also called "contact shoe."

Trolley Wire. On electrified railroads, a term used to describe the overhead wire used to distribute electric current to locomotives or other traction equipment. A more proper term for an overhead electric current distribution system is "catenary."

Truck. The complete assembly of parts including wheels, axles, bearings, side frames, bolster, brake rigging, springs and all associated connecting components, the function of which is to provide support, mobility and guidance to a railroad car.

Truck Bolster. The main transverse member of a truck assembly that transmits car body loads to the side frames through the suspension system. The ends of the bolster fit loosely into the wide openings in the side frames and are retained by the gibs, which contact the side frame column guides. Truck bolster contact with the car body is through the truck center plate, which mates with the body center plate and through the side bearings.

Truck Center Plate. The circular area at the center of a truck bolster, designed to accept the protruding body center plate and provide the principal bearing surface for car body support on the truck bolster. Truck center plates are often fitted with a horizontal wear plate and a vertical wear ring to improve wearing characteristics and extend bolster life.

Truck Centers. On a single car, the distance between the truck center pins as measure along the center sill from the center line of one body bolster to the center line of the other. See Center Pin.

Truck Frame. A structure made of cast steel in one piece, to which the journal boxes or pedestals, springs and other parts are attached, and which forms the skeleton of a truck. One piece truck frames are not generally used for freight cars, but are often found on locomotives and passenger cars.

Truck Hunting. A lateral instability of a truck, generally occurring at high speed, and characterized by one or both wheel sets shifting from side to side with the flanges striking the rail. The resulting motion of the car causes excessive wear in car and truck components, and creates potentially unsafe operating conditions.

Truck Lever. A lever in the truck brake rigging that applies force to the brake beams.

Truck Side. See Side Frame.

Truck Side Bearing. A plate, block, roller or elastic unit fastened to the top surface of a truck bolster on both sides of the center plate, and functioning in conjunction with the body side bearing to support the load of a moving car when variations in track cross level cause the car body to rock transversely on the center plates. See Body Side Bearing, Side Bearing and Side Bearing Roller.

Truck Springs. A general term used to describe any of the several types of springs used in the suspension systems of trucks to provide a degree of vertical cushioning to the car and its load.

Truck Wheel Base. The horizontal distance between the centers of the first and last axles of a truck.

Trunnion. A cylindrical projection on the side of any part that allows a turning or osciliating movement.

Trunk Line. A transportation line operating over an extensive territory.

Truss. An engineering term used to describe a built-up structural frame where the members are straight bars or beams arranged in such a manner that when the structure is loaded, the individual members are theoretically subjected only to tensile or compressive stresses. Some freight car sides are designed as trusses.

Trust Plate. A metal plate attached to a piece of railroad equipment to identify the trustee (usually a bank) holding title to the equipment pursuant to an equipment trust agreement.

Turbocharger. A centrifugal blower driven by an exhaust gas turbine used to supercharge an engine.

Turn-Around Time. The time required to complete the cycle of loading, movement, unloading and placement for reloading of a freight car.

Turnbuckle. An elongated sleeve with a right-hand thread at one end and a left-hand thread at the other for the purpose of tightening the connection between two rods with threaded ends.

Turnout. An arrangement of a switch and a frog with closure rails by means of which rolling stock may be diverted from one track to another. Another name for "track switch."

Turntable. A circular platform with a track section extending across its diameter, pivoted at the center, and used for turning locomotives around at terminals.

Two-Stroke Cycle. The operating cycle of an internal-combustion engine in which there is one power stroke during each revolution of the crankshaft.

U

U-Bolt. A fastening device consisting of a rod bent into the shape of a capital "U" with the straight portions threaded on the ends to accept nuts.

Ultrasonic Inspection. A method for inspection for internal defects in material using ultrasonic sound waves and electronic measuring equipment. Common railroad applications are inspection of axles and wheel rims.

UMLER. Acronym for Universal Machine Language Equipment Register. A computerized file maintained by the Operating Transportation Division of the Association of American Railroads. UMLER contains specific details on internal and external dimensions of equipment as well as special equipment and the general information shown in The Official Railway Equipment Register.

Uncoupling Lever Bracket. A bracket supporting the uncoupling lever on the end of the car.

Uncoupling Lever or Rod. The general term used to describe any of the several types of safety appliance devices used to open the lock on a car coupler when it is desired to separate coupled cars. Uncoupling levers are mounted on the end sill near the side sill to enable manual operation without stepping between the cars.

Undercut. In welding processes, a groove melted into the base metal adjacent to the toe of the weld, and left unfilled by weld metal. Severe undercutting of welded joints results in a weakening of the parent metal, and sets up a potential structural failure.

Undercutter. A device used to remove ballast from under track.

Underframe. The term used to refer to the entire structural framework of the car below the floor, including the center sill, side and end sills, bolsters, cross members, stringers and other attached components.

Uniform System of Accounts. A chart of accounts prescribed by the Interstate Commerce Commission for common and contract carriers. There are separate systems of accounts for the various types of transport under I.C.C. jurisdiction, such as railroads, motor truck and bus lines, freight forwarders, pipe lines, etc.

Unit Train. A train transporting a single commodity from one source (shipper) to one destination (consignee) in accordance with an applicable tariff and with assigned cars.

Universal Joint. A device for connecting the ends of two shafts so as to allow them to have flexibility in every direction within certain defined limits.

Up and Down Rod. A rod used for connecting the semaphore arm to the operating mechanism of a signal. (I.C.C.)

V

"V" Belt. Rubber or composition belts made with tapered sides for gripping pulleys with tapered grooves.

Vacuum. A negative pressure or a suction.

Vacuum Brake. A railroad brake system used mainly outside the United States, actuated by exhausting air from a device on each car to make use of atmospheric air to apply the brakes.

Valve. In its most general sense, any device that opens and closes openings to control flow of a fluid or gas for some purpose. Air brake valves operate in many ways to control flow of air in air brake systems; intake and exhaust valves operate to admit fuel-air mixtures and expel products of combustion in engine cylinders.

Valve Seat. The part of an apparatus in contact with the valve, and which acts with the valve to seal the opening.

Van. See Caboose.

Vent. A small aperture; a hole or passage for air or other fluid to escape.

Ventilated Boxcar. An ordinary boxcar arranged for ventilation and suitable for the transportation of produce or other food stuffs not requiring refrigeration.

Vertical Curve. A curve in the profile of a track to connect intersecting grade lines and to permit the safe and smooth operation of trains over summits and across sags.

Vertical Split Head. A rail defect appearing as a split along or near the middle of the head of a rail and extending into or through the head.

Vertical Strut. One of the three main members of a piggyback trailer hitch. The vertical strut serves to support the weight of a trailer, and has pinned connections at the head, on the deck of the car and at the diagonal strut to enable the entire assembly to be retracted to the deck when not in use.

Vertical Wheel Hand Brake. A type of hand brake mechanism having the hand wheel positioned vertically and mounted on a gear housing which is fastened to the car end. See Horizontal Wheel Hand Brake.

Vestibule. An enclosed space at each end of a passenger car.

Viscosity. A property of a fluid relating to its ability to flow, particularly at low temperatures.

Volt. The unit of electromotive force that, when impressed on an electrical conductor whose resistance is 1 ohm, will produce a current of 1 ampere.

Voltage Drop. The decrease in voltage to a current carrying conductor.

Voltmeter. An instrument for measuring in terms of volts the electromotive force of an electric current.

Volute Spring. A spring made by winding a flat steel strip in a close spiral scroll so that axial movement of the spring is partially restricted by the friction between adjacent coils. Volute springs are sometimes used in spring groups to assist in controlling excessive lateral rocking of cars.

W

Washout. An erosion of the permanent roadbed by storm or flood to such an extent as would cause delay of trains, or endanger traffic.

Washout Nozzle. A removable plug arrangement at the bottom of a tank to facilate cleaning cars with are not permitted to have a bottom unloading valve.

Wasp Excluder. A device for preventing insects from entering openings in air brake equipment where they build obstructions which interfere with the functioning of the equipment.

Water Capacity. The number of gallons of water a tank will hold at a water temperature of 60 degrees Fahrenheit.

Water Jacket. An enclosed space surrounding the cylinder liner of an engine through which water circulates to prevent overheating. Its enclosure may be separate from an integral part of the cylinder liner casting.

Water Pocket (Trackwork). A depression in the roadbed, filled with ballast or other porous material, wherein water collects and is confined.

Water-Tube Boiler. A boiler in which water circulates through tubes surrounded by hot gases which are the products of combustion in the firebox.

Watt. The primary unit of electric power. One watt of power is defined as the amount of energy represented by a current of one ampere flowing through a resistance of one ohm. In direct current (DC) calculations, the product of voltage and amperage is wattage.

Waybill. The primary written documentation of every freight shipment that forms the basis for railroad freight revenue accounts.

Way Car. See Caboose.

Way Switching Tracks. Station, team, industry, and other switching tracks along line of road, on which switching service is performed by road locomotive and crew.

Wearplate. A renewable plate of hardened steel or other material designed for application to the surface of another component exposed to conditions causing severe wear.

Web. In a structural beam such as an "I" beam or channel, the web is the center element between the two flanges. In a built-up beam such as a car center sill, the web plates are the vertical members between the top and bottom cover plates. The web of a rail is the center element between the head and the base.

Weigh Bridge. The track portion of track scales on which a car is spotted for weighing.

Weight Rail. A term generally used in conjunction with car retarder systems to denote a calibrated section of rail, the deflections of which are measured for purpose of determining weight category of cars being classified. Note: the weight information is used to establish ceiling brake shoe pressures and introduce proper information for ultimate speed selection.

Weld. A seam where two members are joined, formed by any of several heating processes resulting in melting and fusing together of the metal on either side of the joint, often with the addition of filler metal to improve the properties of the joint. Welding processes are extremely important in modern car construction.

Welded Rail. Two or more rails welded together at their ends to form a length less than 400 ft. See Continuous Welded Rail (CWR).

Welding Rod. In manual arc welding processes, the term commonly used to refer to the electrode that contacts the pieces to be joined, and is consumed in the welding process. Technically, the term properly refers to filler metal, in wire or rod form, used in any of the several welding processes.

Well Car. A flatcar with a depression or opening in the center to allow the load to extend below the normal floor level when it could not otherwise come within the overhead clearance limits.

Wheel. The specially designed cast or forged steel cylindrical element that rolls on the rail, carries the weight and provides guidance for rail vehicles. Railway wheels are semi-permanently mounted in pairs on steel axles, and are designed with flanges and a tapered tread to provide for operation on track of a specific gage. The wheel also serves as a brake drum on cars with on-tread brakes.

Wheel Base. The horizontal distance between centers of the first and last axles of a locomotive or car.

Wheel Bore. The hole through the hub of the wheel which is machined to precise dimensions to create a press fit on the axle wheel seat.

Wheel Flange. The tapered projection extending completely around the inner rim of a railway wheel, the function of which, in conjunction with the flange of a mate wheel, is to keep the wheel set on the track by limiting lateral movement of the assembly against the inside surface of either rail.

Wheel Grinding. A process of refining the tread contour of steel railway wheels by rotating them against a grinding wheel under precise controls.

Wheel Plate. The part of a railway wheel between the hub and the rim.

Wheel Press. A machine to mount railway wheels on car or locomotive axles. Wheel presses are required to be equipped with pressure recording mechanisms to assure compliance with mandatory rules governing wheel mounting practice.

Wheel Report. A listing of the cars in a train as it leaves a yard, made from waybills, on which the conductor posts set-offs and pickups.

Wheel Seat. That portion of a car or locomotive axle that fits into the wheel bore. The wheel seat is machined to precise tolerances to create a press fit requiring specified pressures to accomplish the mounting operation.

Wheel Set. The term used to describe a pair of wheels mounted on an axle.

Wheel Slip Relay. An electrical device which senses a slipping wheel, and causes a reduction of power, provides automatic sanding and activates a wheel slip indicator in the locomotive cab.

Wheel Tread. The slightly tapered or sometimes cylindrical circumferential surface of a railway wheel that bears on the rail and serves as a brake drum on cars with conventional truck brake rigging. See Tread.

Wheel Truing Brake Shoe. A special brake shoe with abrasive inserts to grind the wheel tread and flange to true contour when brake applications are made in service.

Wide Gage. A track defect characterized by the rails having spread to a dimension in excess of the standard 4' 8-1/2" dimension between the inside heads. A combination of wide gage track and a wheel set with minimum back to back distance between wheels could cause a derailment. The term "wide gage" or "broad gage" is also sometimes used to refer to railroads built to gages wider than standard, such as 5 ft.

Wing Fence. A fence connecting the apron of the stockguard with the right-of-way or line fence.

Wire Chase. A casing used to protect electrical conductors in a building.

Wire Gage. A gage for measuring the diameter of electric wire.

Wire Gauze. Wire woven into gauze having a fine mesh.

Work Train. A train engaged in company service for which no revenue is received, such as official, inspection, and pay trains; trains running special with fire apparatus to save the carrier's property from destruction; and trains distributing ballast, bridge material or other material and supplies for maintenance or for additions and betterments.

Wrecking Crane. A heavy self-propelled crane mounted on rail trucks, usually powered by a Diesel engine for use in cleaning up wrecks. Frequently called "wrecker."

Wrecking Frog. A device having one end elevated to form an inclined plane by which derailed trucks can be replaced on the track. Also commonly called "car replacers" or "re-railers."

Wrought Steel Wheel. A railway wheel made by hot forging and rolling as opposed to the pressure casting process.

Wye. A term used to describe a track arrangement shaped like the letter "Y" but with a connecting segment between the two upper legs. This track layout is often used in small yards and at some rip tracks to enable equipment to be turned without a turntable.

Y

Yard. A system of tracks within defined limits provided for the making up of trains, storing of cars and other purposes.

Yard Engine. An engine assigned to yard service and working wholly within yard limits.

Yard Lead. An extended track connecting either end of a yard with the main track.

Yardmaster. The railroad employee designated as being in charge of all operations in a yard.

Yard Office. A building in terminal yards to provide office accommodations for the yardmaster and office personnel.

Yard Speed. A speed that will permit stopping within one-half the range of vision. (Standard Code)

Yellow Eye. A slang term used to describe a yellow signal.

Yoke. The component in a railroad car draft system that transits longitudinal coupler forces to the draft gear. See Coupler Yoke.

Z

Zee Section. A commercial rolled steel structural member, so called because of the shape of its cross section. Zee sections are often used a floor stringers in box and gondola car construction.

Zinc Chromate. The rust-inhibiting ingredient contained in many commercial prime paints.